# ENGAGING Practices

# ENGAGING
# Practices

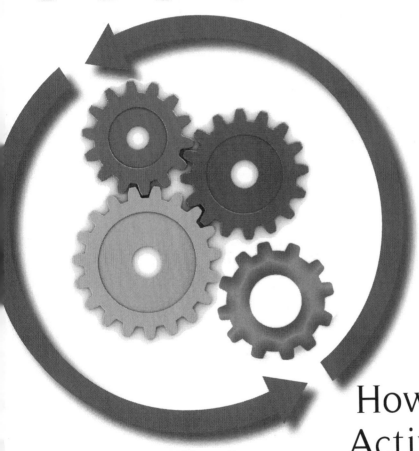

Cristal L. McGill, Ph.D.

How to
Activate
Student
Learning

Engaging Practices: How to Activate Student Learning
Published by White Water Publishing
Colorado Springs, Colorado

Library of Congress Control Number: 2017911629
McGILL, CRISTAL, Author
Engaging Practices
Cristal McGill, Ph.D.

ISBN: 978-0-9991027-0-1

EDUCATION / Teaching Methods & Materials / General
EDUCATION / Professional Development

QUANTITY PURCHASES: Schools, companies, professional groups, clubs, and other organizations may qualify for special terms when ordering quantities of this title. For information, email Info@WhiteWaterPublishing.net.

WHITE WATER
PUBLISHING

To Jennifer who challenges me,
helps me grow, and is my wizard.
To my mom for her never-ending support and belief in me,
and to my exceptional friend Rich Allen
with all the respect that he deserves.

"Teaching is a creative profession. Teaching, properly conceived, is not a delivery system. You know, you're not there just to pass on received information. Great teachers do that, but what great teachers also do is mentor, stimulate, provoke, engage. You see, in the end, education is about learning. If there's no learning going on, there's no education going on."

Sir Ken Robinson, TED Talk:
*"How to Escape Education's Death Valley,"* 2013

# TABLE OF CONTENTS

# Introduction

The guiding philosophy behind *Engaging Practices* is to weave a variety of engagement principles into your everyday teaching repertoire. Engaging practices are defined by the degree of attention, curiosity, interest, optimism, and passion that your students display when they are learning or being instructed. We all know that learning improves when students are inquisitive, interested, or inspired; learning  tends to suffer when students are bored, dispassionate, disaffected, or otherwise disengaged. I have yet to meet a teacher who wants to be boring.

I invite you to dive into a teaching philosophy rich with facilitative tips and methods that pay huge dividends in authentic engagement. All teaching levels—elementary school, middle school, high school, and tertiary levels—benefit from adopting an engaging mindset. The payoff is your students want to be in your class, participate in classroom instruction, and want to learn.

The engaging strategies in this book offer a unique balance of instructional student-centered approaches with delivery techniques that improve cooperation and joy and engage learners. Once I began incorporating these strategies and techniques into my classrooms, I experienced higher levels of interest, cooperation, and better relationships.

When I used these engagement practices while teaching at the university level, my students reported that they looked forward to coming to my class. At the graduate level, my lead professor shared with me that compared to students who did not take my classes, my students demonstrated a better understanding of learning theory as evidenced in their thesis-writing projects.

Using an engaging practices approach, we consciously develop our skills as teachers in ways that help students thrive. Your students' energy in the classroom moves like a river. As students engage, interact in groups, and move from topic to topic, the collective energy of the room ebbs and flows. The energy is dynamic. Stopping the river is a major undertaking, but redirecting the flow is more efficient. Encouragement and redirection keep the energy flowing. Knowing and capitalizing on this classroom ebb and flow are skills we manage day to day, and are the centerpiece of the Engagement Model presented in this book.

The skills incorporated in this guiding framework will refresh your teaching and drive daily decisions you make while teaching your students. In return, you re-energize your own teaching.

This book's Engagement Model, a blueprint if you will, helps you plan and execute a whole new level of student engagement. When we use these techniques in the classroom, we become teachers who encourage, inspire, and motivate. It is through our relationships, our thoughtful word choice, and the adjustments we make to meet students' needs that give us our vitality. Engaging practices in the classroom are supported with a practical and important model. Paying attention to all parts of this model provides responsiveness in our students. Let's face it, we have the potential to turn students "on" or "off." We can develop our skills to support positive relationships, and in turn, encourage students to actively participate. These skills also foster interest and curiosity. The Engagement Model is a visual representation of the many moving parts of this orchestrated philosophy.

Everything we do matters. Our energy affects our students' energy. Like a dance, we continuously synchronize our energy with our learners. We strive to be engaging, effective, motivating teachers. Our ability to communicate, in combination with an effective pedagogy, provides a powerful experience for all our students.

The truth is we all want to be part of something big and exciting, to have a larger purpose. We can structure our content around these drives to create enthusiasm. We are the "excited link." Our ability to connect authentically, our every action, thought, and word, propel our students beyond apathy and indifference.

Let's delight our students with our passions, joyously foster their ideas, connect with their hearts, and inspire their actions. Ignite agreeable change in your classrooms and make the learning process thrilling. As teachers we are the catalysts of growth, learning, and change.

*I have come to a frightening conclusion.*

*I am the decisive element that creates the climate.*

*It is my personal approach that creates the climate.*

*It is my daily mood that makes the weather.*

*As a teacher, I possess tremendous power to make a child's life miserable or joyous.*

*I can be a tool of torture or an instrument of inspiration.*

*I can humiliate or humor, hurt or heal.*

*In all situations, it is my response that decides whether a crisis will be escalated or de-escalated, and a child humanized or de-humanized.*

- Hiam Ginott

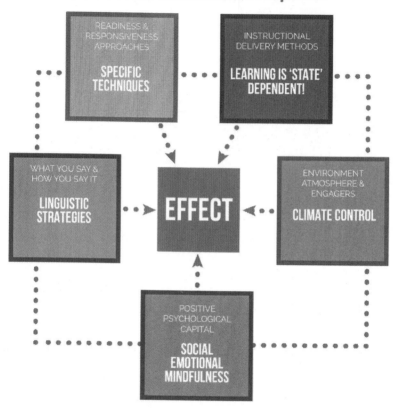

## Overview of the Engagement Model

This engagement model includes five different components that, when orchestrated together, create an enriched learning climate. Each component stands on its own merits, but when combined, you experience an involved (hand-raising), energetic, participating group of learners.

The following pages contain a high-level overview of the model with a brief synopsis of each component that is explained in greater detail in the subsequent chapters. This gives you a snap shot big picture view of the engagement model.

# LEARNING IS "STATE" DEPENDENT: INSTRUCTIONAL DELIVERY METHODS

We promote engagement in three ways with our instructional delivery methods: state changes, use of music, and giving effective directions.

## State changes

The ability to learn is a state of mind. State management is an instructional method that retains students' attention in an optimal learning state. Keeping students' attention levels refreshed and focused means that you keep learning at the crest of the wave, as we'll discuss in Chapter 1.

## Using music in the classroom

We use music for many reasons, but there are very strategic ways to use music that help manage a classroom. Using music enhances the mood and energy of learners. It helps create a buffer of white noise during group or silent work to aid students' ability to focus on the task at hand. It can also be used effectively during state changes and transitions for movement. Music is powerful.

## Giving effective directions

Giving effective directions is as much an art as it is a staple in educational pedagogy. The "art" of giving directions is more about personal discipline. Additionally, we are conditioning our students for ideal responsiveness and task completion. Perfecting the art of effectively giving directions is a necessary skill that aids instruction and student comprehension of the task assignment. The way you give directions is the difference between getting the students on task quickly and effortlessly or having to repeat yourself several times and re-explain the task at hand.

## TURN IT UP! CLIMATE CONTROL

We turn up the climate by creating an inviting environment, appealing atmosphere, and using engagers.

### Environment and atmosphere

Climate control speaks directly to the arrangement of the room, visual support, live plants, natural light, technology, and class seating. The psychological atmosphere in the room is promoted by the positive teacher tone, display of posters, word walls, cleanliness, and visual organization. Attending to the climate with a visually pleasing environment, cosmetic as it sounds, promotes respect for the learning space and lends itself to the comfort of learners. We purposely organize our space, plan different classroom layouts, and adjust resource availability depending on our learning goals. Classrooms may change day-to-day, or week-to-week.

### Using engagers

An engager is quick, fun activity to liven up your students when their energy is waning and their motivation is decreasing.

We use engagers to provide opportunities to stimulate and/or re-stimulate students. Engagers can also offer personal development occasions to grow social-emotional skills. Using engagers throughout our teaching day creates chances for students to empower friendships, practice new skills, and negotiate relationship development. Delivering an energy infusion lifts the mood, allowing students to experience the content with a refreshed mindset, and reducing behavior problems before they start.

# SOCIAL-EMOTIONAL MINDFULNESS: POSITIVE PSYCHOLOGICAL CAPITAL & RAPPORT

We build our social-emotional assets by focusing on positive psychological capital, and cultivating our rapport skills.

> "Seek first to understand, then to be understood."
> - Steven R. Covey

### Social-emotional mindfulness

Social-emotional mindfulness is the soft skill knowledge we use to understand and manage emotions, feel and show empathy for others, establish and maintain positive relationships, and make responsible decisions.[1]

When we consciously address our learner's social-emotional abilities, we promote soft skill opportunities for our learners to improve their personal self-awareness, social awareness, self-control, and relationship skills. The stronger our students' soft skills develop, the more gains we experience as teachers.

### Positive psychological capital (PsyCap)

Positive psychological capital is likened to a savings account that supports the consequences of negative or negatively-perceived human interactions. Development of social and emotional assets builds psychological capital that endows students with the mental strength to cope with adversity. Academic stressors threaten psychological and physical well-being. These stressors may contribute to problems including distraction, fatigue, anxiety, and even illness. Learners with stress-resilient personalities suffer less in response to the same stresses. Barbara Fredrickson, a champion in the field of positive psychology, has studied the effects of mild positive emotions on desired cognitive traits, including attentiveness and problem-solving. Fredrickson found that feeling a mild and pleasant positive emotional state before experiencing content leads to greater retention.[2]

### Rapport and relationships

Strong relationships are the bedrock for growing and inspiring young minds. You can enrich any learning environment by building personal rapport. Your authentic relationships improve your approachability, making you less threatening and cultivating a safe place for students to risk failure. We nurture emotionally healthy settings by purposefully facilitating positive relationships *with* and *among* our learners.

## LINGUISTIC STRATEGIES: WHAT AND HOW YOU SAY IT! FRAMING AND CURIOSITY

Language is a teacher's most powerful tool. Every day, the words, tone, and pace we choose have the power to help students develop self-control, build their sense of belonging, and gain understanding.

We use linguistic strategies with framing language to create relevance toward content, and curiosity strategies to create inquisitive and interested learners.

### Mindful language—what and how you say it

Engagement is social! We cultivate it with our invitations, feedback, and mindful word choice to promote interested learners. We use linguistic tools like frames, open loops, and positioning statements to guide students' focus. Carefully crafted statements influence attitude, curiosity, compliance, and relevance to the content. Like a filter placed on a camera to create an effect, how we say *everything* fundamentally influences a leaner's attitude. We can foster a desire to belong and be an active participant in any learning. Linguistic strategies command the students' full attention and result in higher levels of interaction.

## SPECIFIC TECHNIQUES: RESPONSIVE AND READINESS APPROACHES

Specific techniques are the subtle and explicit details that create a symphony of reactions. These details are a series of methods that increase quicker student responses, student inclusion, and questioning strategies that set students up for success. They are the specifics that improve student participation and improve the overall engagement. The specific techniques listed in Chapter 5 are the tweaks or hacks in instruction that help your students to be responsive and ready to participate easily.

### Responsive and readiness approaches

Specific techniques can increase student responsiveness, promote autonomy, simplify tasks, and improve group dynamics. Many of these techniques accelerate responsiveness and active learning. And while they may seem like common sense in practice, sometimes they are not so common. Many of these specific details add to our effectiveness as teachers, lending merit to our work, and stimulating engagement. You will be armed with a repertoire of teaching moves that foster resiliency and mastery in all learners.

### Is Your Teaching Memorable?

In addition to the Engagement Model, two chapters add finishing touches to your engaging practices. In Chapter 6, we discuss strategies to make your teaching memorable. Knowing how to make information memorable is one of a teacher's most potent secret weapons.

There are many memory strategies that we can use to increase recall. These include powerful mnemonic strategies and elaborative rehearsal techniques. One important aspect of memory, often undervalued, is that memory is the art of attention. Your students learn what they remember, so give them the tools to remember.

### Lesson Design and Planning

If you believe in these engaging practices, you will want a structure that helps you implement the strategies into your learning designs. In Chapter 7 you will see the five-part implementation model that serves as a basic guide to help incorporate these strategies into an orchestrated approach. Also included are key debriefing and processing techniques to help you summarize important learning for your students.

Be sure to check out my personal note to you along with the appendices loaded with music planning tips, lists of engagers, summary activities, generating social-emotional opportunity lists, and creative debriefing options.

# Learning is "State" Dependent: Instructional Delivery Methods

My intentions are to persuade you to examine your personal instructional delivery strategies. "State" dependent instructional delivery methods will increase your students' ability to pay attention to your instruction or lectures more effectively. We'll discuss evidence that recommends certain methods, and the theory behind them. After this, I'll arm you with practical, easy strategies that support your adoption of these engaging practices. Some of these ideas will resonate with you; others may not fit your disposition. Embrace what works and leave the rest.

These ideas are appropriate for all age levels and great for students' knowledge retention. More importantly, these engaging practices will grow your own resilience in your career. Remember, what you give to your students, you give back to yourself in energy and satisfaction. You don't have to believe me now, just try a couple methods at a time and notice the upgraded student engagement!

Part of teaching with an engaging practices approach is that we focus on our students' needs first, such as their physical comfort, energy, attitude, distractions, and the like. Then, and only then, can we deliver content. Students who are unfocused, uncomfortable, or distracted are not in an optimal learning mindset for recall or comprehension of instructional delivery. Focus on teaching people first, and then you can deliver content.

## PEOPLE FIRST, THEN CONTENT

Traditional teaching includes face-to-face instruction, PowerPoint, document cameras, and interactive whiteboards where learners are in a "sit and get" format of instruction. Most of you who have the job of educating others are good at what you do. In fact, many of you have moved away from lecture-based methods and work to involve your learners in a variety of ways. New curriculum demands tug at your time; you must incorporate twenty-first century skills and grow your students' social, emotional, personal, and interpersonal life skills. Meeting all these challenges takes precious time. Often, we jump right into our content due to time constraints and outside pressure to have the whole class meet specific performance targets. When we succumb to the pressures and neglect the human need effect, we often sacrifice all the invisible objectives of personal learning. When we focus on people first we have bonus upshots.

The experience is positive for both you and your learner. You will find that your students retain more information, engage in richer dialogue, and you cover more content. Keeping it personal and responsive to the needs of the group fosters a safe, trusting environment.

When the focus is on people first, ask these questions:

- Are my students physically and socially comfortable?
- Can learners see how the content is relevant to them personally?
- Have I created a sense of psychological safety?

The focus on people first requires a shift in thinking away from the typical sole focus on simply teaching content. When we teach to basic human needs *first*, covering the content part is easy.

## CREST OF THE WAVE—ATTENTION SPANS

How long can you pay attention?

Let's define paying attention. Paying attention means you can recall the information and retain it for later use. It looks like students sitting tall, listening and nodding, participating, taking notes, and demonstrating interest.

Generally speaking, attention levels wax and wane per individual. We compete for our students' attention and engagement level during instructional delivery. Bunce, et al.[3] studied patterns of student inattention and mind wandering and found several reasons it may be important to break up lectures and refresh attention. The study was conducted in three different undergraduate chemistry courses. Students in those courses used clickers to self-report (to the research team, not the course teacher) lapses in their attention. After each lapse, students pressed one of three buttons on the clickers: one button to indicate a lapse of a minute or less, another button for lapses of two to three minutes, and a third button for a lapse of five minutes or longer.

There was an observed pattern of first spike in attention lapses just thirty seconds into the lecture segment. The next consistent spike in reported attention lapses occurred at 4.5 to 5.5 minutes into the lecture, followed by another spike at 7 to 9 minutes, and another at 9 to

10 minutes into the lecture. This pattern continued throughout the lecture with attention lapses occurring more frequently as the lecture progressed. By the end of the lecture, lapses occurred about every two minutes.[4]

Students consistently reported fewer lapses when teachers were using "nonlecture pedagogies," including things like demonstrations, group work, and clicker questions. This result confirms well-established findings that students are more engaged and attentive when they are doing something other than listening to the teacher lecture.

The teaching implications of this research are clear. Teachers should try to improve student attentiveness by using a variety of instructional approaches, especially those that actively engage students. These approaches enable students to engage with the content in different formats and make it easier for them to pay attention after the activity has ended.

It is reasonable to expect brief lapses in student attention. Incorporating active learning strategies, especially those of brief state changes, is a proactive way to battle the attention waxing and waning, mind-wandering struggle.

Knowing when to respond to students' attention levels can be described as reading the room and reacting to the inertia of their engagement level. Much like ocean waves building, peaking, and crashing down, there are swells and crests in the learning environment. When the students' ability to draw useful learning from a given mode of instruction has peaked, we've reached the "crest of the wave." This metaphor was coined by Rich Allen, Ph.D.[5] At this point it is in the best interests of both you and the students to move to an alternative form of interaction, to engage in a change in the instruction that will recapture their focus and interest.

These questions will drive your decisions:

- What is the sound level?
- Are the students on or off task?
- Are they sitting on the edge of their seats or rocking back and forth?
- What is the energy level?
- Is it time for a change of pace?
- Do learners need to move around or take a break?

These are the questions that guide teaching moment by moment. If these vital cues get ignored the students may grow increasingly uncomfortable, impatient, hesitant, restless, and even resistant. You need to be consistently responsive to the "waves" of interest or disinterest in the room.

Even when the environmental factors that impact a class are perfect, the room temperature is comfortable, desks are in the best arrangement, and the type of technology being used is working, the question remains: How long can your students pay attention?

While answers will always vary among individuals and situations, my experience is that adults can fully pay attention in new learning situations for about fifteen minutes at a time, before they kick into a skill they learned in high school; they have learned to fake paying attention. Digital devices (smartphones, tablets, laptops) have complicated how adults and young adults pay attention. See recent data on how watching television has changed the way we receive information in Figure 1 below.

> 1. How long is the average length of a TV drama, comedy, news, or documentary before a commercial break?
>    A. About 20 minutes
>    B. About 5-9 minutes
>    C. About 8-12 minutes
>    D. Not long enough
> 2. How long are the commercial breaks between segments?
>    A. They feel like forever.
>    B. Probably around 15 minutes
>    C. Closer to 8 minutes
>    D. About 4-6 transcriptions
>
> *Answer: If you circled 1C and 2C & D, yep congratulations!*

Figure 1: Television and our attention span[6]

Why the TV analogy?[7] According to the Nielsen ratings firm, the number of commercials in a typical hour of television has grown to about 14 minutes and 15 seconds.[8] In *The Ten-Minute Trainer*, Bowman says we have become conditioned to expect fast-paced, attention-getting methods of information delivery, which reinforces the power of the image to teach, entertain, convince, and make a message memorable. Since the first commercial break in television is around ten minutes into the programming, it has set up expectations of faster-paced information delivery along with rich imagery.

So where does this leave us?

Cultivate your engagement meter by being acutely aware of your students' attention patterns and whether they are engaged in their tasks. You should provide strategic, brief energy breaks every ten to fifteen minutes; sooner if you sense the room beginning to "crest." Given the volume of information teachers must deliver, it's tempting to continue to speak beyond students' capacity to absorb any more information. Discipline yourself to respect the energy crest and honor the need of your learners by having them talk in a pair share or read, edit notes, brainstorm, or use digital support. As a result, everyone comes back to new instruction refreshed. Everyone!

*Definition:*
*A state change occurs when a teacher changes the method of instruction for the class from one modality to another. Generally, state changes are brief, perhaps less than 30 seconds*

## ALL LEARNING IS "STATE" DEPENDENT

All learning is "state dependent." In other words, learning is embedded in an emotional-psychological condition.[9] When you recognize a waning attention span in a particular circumstance, change something in your instructional delivery. By doing this, you change the state of your learners. The word "state" in this situation refers to the student's physiology—their physical and mental being as measured by their engagement level. "State change" is the expression commonly used in active learning environments. Generally, state changes are brief, perhaps less than thirty seconds. When you use state changes, you engage students, refresh their focus, and consistently "make easy" their readiness and ability to learn.

We observe students "state" as demonstrated by their behaviors in any given moment. Their state includes their feelings, thoughts, sensations, physiology, and body all at once. Each of our states (hunger, excitement, confidence, curiosity, etc.) has its own possibilities and constraints. Movement is crucial to every brain function, including memory, emotion, language, and learning. It is obvious that having your students sit quietly in rows is a worst-case scenario for the brain. What the brain needs is active participation from its partner the body.

Let's look at what boredom may occasionally look like. We have all seen it, right? The mind-body connection provides insight: when the body moves, the mind moves. What your students feel and think manifests in their body language. We've seen bored students slumping or lying back in chairs or collapsed over their desks. Enticing students to sit tall, put both feet on the floor, and lean forward changes the body posture. This simple adjustment puts learners in a more attentive, alert physical state.

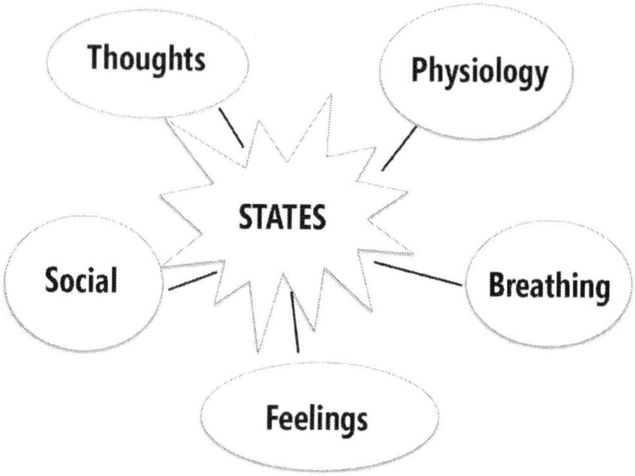

Figure 2: Learner States

A state change in a learning environment causes the mind to refocus attention on what is happening. For brief periods of time, students will feel like starting something new, a condition in which the brain tends to be in a heightened level of awareness.[10] Using well-spaced and sometimes frequent state changes can help students maintain high levels of attention.

Positive group redirection is always top choice for influencing behavior through action. A positive emotional state is valuable for several reasons. An increased positive affect leads to improved flexibility in behavior and judgment.[11] Positive emotional states are what we are striving to achieve. As we experience positive learning states, we feel uplifting feelings. Mihaly Csikszentmihalyi[12] describes "flow" as the psychology of the optimal experience. He states that when we feel this flow we feel a sense of exhilaration; a deep sense of enjoyment that is cherished and becomes a landmark in memory for what life should be like.

From a practicality point, students who experience positive feelings at school will associate these positive feelings with learning, you as a teacher, and school in general. They may help strengthen attendance, follow through, and student effort.

In his book, *Teaching with the Brain in Mind,* Eric Jensen refers to using state changes as motivation for engagement. State changes motivate and influence our students' decisions. Evoking noticeable positive emotional states gives learners more freedom to make new discoveries. This adds to the social-emotional learning opportunities within content delivery and keeps it as a subtle learning objective.

When you make strategic changes in your instructional delivery that encourage reflection, community development, and learning, this is the use of a state change. You assist your learners in accessing an optimal learning state of focused concentration. Your skill in facilitating the state of your learners is directly proportionate to their ability to stay engaged. Managing the flow of your instructional state changes becomes routine and automatic the more you use them.

There are countless ways in which state changes can be accomplished. For example, after a brief lecture or lesson, switching students to small group discussion is a state change. Moving from small to large group discussions would be another state change. Use of humor and laughter is a state change. State changes can be subtle, such as vocal changes or moving from direct instruction mode into telling a story. State changes can also be quite dramatic, such as finding a new place to sit in the class, or being indoors for one section of the class and moving outdoors for the next.

Using contrast is a subtle way to cause a state change, especially with older learners. Let me elaborate. In a single classroom session, you will say many things. Central ideas can be highlighted for students by creating a contrast in their experience. Creating contrast is symbolically comparable to bolded, italicized, or underlined words in text. Build in dramatic pauses or make quotation marks with your fingers to accentuate what you are saying—these are examples of contrast. If you have a quiet, focused, academic-driven portion of instruction, follow it with an energetic, movement-oriented activity. Both become unique in comparison to each other. Using contrast as a subtle state change creates a distinctive, fluid learning environment rich with appealing experiences.

The principles of teaching people first, then content, using state changes, and responding to the crest of the wave are essential to building an instructional flow and getting the results you intend. They allow you to engage focused and refreshed learners.

Your ability to be consistent lays the groundwork for, and gives your full attention to, higher levels of interaction and high-quality discussion, projects, routines, and procedures.

You can even use state management to address minor behavior disruptions, such as students talking to their neighbors, distracting others around them, or not participating. You can influence behavior and refocus attention through an action of instructing students to thank their peers, give them applause, or give their seatmate a high-five or fist bump. The intention is to determine if the state that you are seeing is appropriate for the next target behavior you want. For example, if your students are in a high-energy state you might consider a breathing technique to elicit a calmer more focused state for the next lesson segment. Change the state and you change the behavior.

There are many ways to incorporate state changes into your instructional delivery. Below are a few categories of state changes to help you expand your knowledge and inspire your imagination. They work with all age groups; you need only to keep in mind suitability. Remember, a state change is generally brief, perhaps less than thirty seconds. You'll want to develop a cadre of ideas. The variety is not only for your students but also for your own resilience and endurance. Keeping it fresh keeps the energy light, playful, and creative.

**Categories of State Changes**

*Novelty*

The very nature of novelty is new and different. This category of state change invites playfulness and promotes a fresh and unique flavor to demonstrations. Check out these examples: Hold up an object in your hands, change the lighting in the room, or do a simple magic trick, perhaps one that illustrates a certain point related to the content.

---

**Categories of State Changes to Consider:**

*Novelty*
Visual cues
Storytelling
Auditory Environment
Ownership
*Physical Space*
HUMOR
Social Interaction
Distribution of Resources
*Discuss it Standing*

---

Figure 3: State Change Categories

### Visual cues

Decorative bulletin boards and digital media are a given. The use of prepared flip charts with visual cues, directional signs, colored paper used as visual prompts, and posters can increase anticipation and engagement.

### Storytelling

The use of stories is the skill of finding the "twist" that enables us to illustrate and highlight key points related to the content being taught. Almost every story worth its salt has an important lesson buried somewhere within. The question is, can you, the teacher, find the useful lesson within a particular story? Learning to find the twist in each story so it can become useful within a classroom context is a valuable skill all by itself.

### Auditory environment

Beyond the use of music as an auditory emotional tool (discussed below and in Chapter 2), you can use several auditory methods to bring students' attention back to instruction or further directions as needed. Paired shares, gallery walks, or other cooperative learning initiatives and stations are a great way to use audio tools like chimes and toy train whistles. Changing your vocal pacing, tone, and pitch also serves as an auditory state change.

### Ownership

The power of built-in opportunities for choice and ownership is uniquely important to developing a socially emotional safe environment, not to mention a necessary ingredient for intrinsic motivation. Occasionally, ownership can be as simple as allowing the students to choose who goes first in a pair share assignment. Adding another layer to ownership could be to allow the students to choose the order of the content objectives being instructed and when to experience the activity that may be used at the beginning, middle, or end of the hour.

## Physical Space

How we arrange the classroom—seating, lighting, use of visuals, live plants, books, stuffed animals, props for learning objectives—can serve as a subtle state change.

## Humor

> "A sense of humor...is needed armor.
> Joy in one's heart and some laughter on one's lips is a sign that the person down deep has a pretty good grasp of life."
> - Hugh Sidey

Humor can relieve monotony, helping students stay engaged. Humor is a motivator. It helps bring students to class and keeps them coming back. Students who enjoy class are more likely to be engaged and actively participate, providing a win-win for both students and teachers. Laughter brings students together both physically and psychologically. It fosters friendships and promotes a positive sense of belonging. Strategic use can help quell the multiple pressures facing teachers and students every day.

Many people have had bad experiences with humor in the teaching environment. While people love to laugh at a joke, they don't want to be one. Keep interactions playful and meaningful to create a learning environment that is based on emotional security and mutual respect. "If just once in a month, or even once in a school year, we choose to make a **sarcastic comment** or **cutting remark** to a student or staff member, we may as well have carved it in stone. They may pretend to have forgotten that moment, but they will never forget it."[13] Keep humor fun and not at anyone else's expense.

### Social Interaction

Social interactions are the glue to an invested class and engaged students. Building purposeful social state changes into the class flow can disrupt and redirect much misbehavior.

### Distribution of resources

Distributing resources is a perfect time for a state change during the flow of class instruction. It offers an opportunity for social interaction and physical (physiological) movement, and a chance for a novel way for students to gather the resources needed for an assignment. Examples of this state change include placing papers around symbolically like a scavenger hunt, occasionally tossing out pens or papers, or building in group leader rituals to collect activity resources or class assignments.

### Discuss it standing

Although this one seems obvious, it isn't usually capitalized upon. If students are seated for a paired share or cooperative learning activity, mix it up. Instruct them to stand in a group or pair with a different student. You might also ask them to walk and talk. This is a great opportunity to add minimal, simple-to-implement movement and still manage the content delivery of the classroom.

I use state changes to manage the flow of content delivery and refresh the focus and the attention level of my students. This notion of pacing and flow keeps interest level high and engagement varied. State changes are the mechanics we use to manage the energy of the class with the content being delivered. Reading the room and the attention level of the students is the most significant sign of when to use a state change. A typical rule of thumb when reading the crest of the wave is to consider implementing a state change every ten to fifteen minutes.

We get to spend a year with our students and the way we deliver content, instructions, and give feedback can make for a long, arduous year or a dynamic, exciting, fun year for all (including the teacher). Can you imagine the necessity of their and our energy management to keep it fresh and novel? Reading and reacting to your students' energy dynamics in the classroom means part responding and part creating a vibrant energy flow. Alter your state changes by occasionally rotating partners and changing up your students' modes of response. The first time you ask them to turn to a partner and share, you'll feel a fresh energy in the room. The sixth time in a row you will be likely to hear heavy sighs. Keep it varied!

# USE MUSIC AS A TOOL

*"Take a music bath once or twice a week, for music is to the soul what water is to the body."* - Oliver Wendall Holmes

Harvard psychologist Howard Gardner says that we each have a preferred learning modality. Effective lessons must be not just auditory, or visual, or kinesthetic, but multi-sensory. Multi-sensory experiences light up more of the brain, leading to greater retention.[14]

**Every kind** of music is **good**... except the boring kind

The following pages offer suggestions for when, how, and why to use music during your classes. With these techniques, you, the teacher, not only increase your students' involvement in the classroom, but add to your own energy as well. Music aids in learning because it enhances the emotional experience.

Music has the ability to alter your student's mental and even physiological state. Have you ever felt weary or uninspired, put on a favorite upbeat tune, and suddenly found yourself tapping your foot, swaying, or even dancing? This is the result for many of your learners when you use music strategically.

Like language, music has its own vocabulary and grammar. These language skills and music also utilize similar neural pathways. Animals can perceive music, even if they've never been exposed to it before.

It appears that music rewards the listener to the degree that the music is found to be pleasant. Many studies suggest that the right music can influence dopamine, the brain's reward neurotransmitter. The beauty of this is that classroom learning can get associated with positive emotions. Positive emotional learning supports long-term memory. When positive emotions are associated with school, our students tend to come to class on time, participate frequently, and generally invest time in assignments.

Unlike a tangible reward, music can arouse feelings of euphoria and pleasure. Scientists used PET scans and found endogenous dopamine release at peak emotional arousal during music listening.[15] Salimpoor suggests that the time course of a dopamine release was also interesting; dopamine was more involved during anticipation of the music, and then again at the experience of peak emotional responses.

Even the anticipation of an abstract reward, such as listening to music for pleasure, can result in a dopamine release. In teacher terms, this gives us an edge in supporting working memory and positive emotional connections to learning.

Music is powerful! The intentional use of music in the classroom sets the atmosphere to enhance our teaching and learning activities. The use of music for learning makes the process much more engaging and interesting for students and for us. Appropriate music creates a positive learning atmosphere and encourages students to feel comfortable participating. In this way it also has a great effect upon students' attitudes and motivation to learn. Music promotes, changes, calms, and manages the ideal learning state of students.

BOB LIKED THE IDEA OF MUSIC IN HIS CLASSROOM

It turns out using music in the classroom can also be messy. Not all students respond to music in the same way. I have accidently used music that was too slow, and it impacted students' participation (and complaint) levels. This may seem obvious, but some types of music can have a negative effect on our students, such as heavy rock and roll, music with a downbeat, and music with profane or violent lyrics.

Music facilitates the attainment of flow, a highly desirable mental state in which all distractions appear to fade away and people feel fully engaged, focused, and energized. Artists crave flow because it seems to be the state during which creativity flows from its deepest wellspring. But flow applies to virtually any task that requires full attention and concentration.

If you make less-than-desirable music choices—too slow, too old, or unpopular—the good news is you can just change the song and recover quickly. In Chapter 2 and the Appendix, I give concrete suggestions on how to make appropriate music selections.

In general, music with certain rhythms helps us feel better. Familiar music we have enjoyed in the past reactivates those positive feelings. High-energy music activates our brain's "uppers," norepinephrine and dopamine. Below are studies by Kniffn et.al. about music and cooperation.

In the first of two studies, 78 participants were randomly divided into two groups: a "happy music" group that heard songs like "Yellow Submarine" by The Beatles and the theme from the television show "Happy Days," and an "unhappy music" group that heard less familiar heavy metal songs like "Smokahontas" by Attack Attack!

The participants in each group used a computer application in which they played a sort of a token economy with other unidentified participants in the same space, but players didn't speak to each other.

In the study, each person was given 10 tokens corresponding to monetary value and was paired with two other people. They participated in more than 20 rounds of decision-making. After each round each person was prompted to either keep their tokens or allocate them to a group pool which would be split among the participants at the end. Tokens in the group pool were valued 1.5 times as much as those held individually.

Consistently, people listening to happy music contributed more to the group pool.

In a second study, the researchers repeated the design with an added no-music group, and also measured the participant's moods.

Again, those hearing happy music contributed more to the group pool than those hearing unhappy music or no music at all. Unhappy music elicited a worse mood than both other conditions, and happier mood was tied to more token contributions to the group.[16]

Learning how to activate these positive feelings is part of every good teacher's job. The payoff is twofold. Our learners benefit from music's influence on their affect, which in turn boosts our affect.

I experience the same uplift when I use music in my classrooms; it reenergizes me and keeps me in an upbeat zone. It helps me to be responsive and flexible to the ever-changing classroom demands.

Your use of music and state changes can be limited or enhanced by the way you give directions. Master the art of giving directions and drastically reduce your need to repeat yourself.

# BUFF UP YOUR DIRECTION–GIVING AND FACILITATION SKILLS

*"Providing clear directions for learners is the golden key to successful teaching."* - Rich Allen, Ph.D.

One of the least-appreciated concepts in all of teaching is the art of giving effective directions. And much like a seemingly simple work of art, they may be more difficult to create than they first appear. To ensure maximum efficiency when giving directions, teachers may want to consider these basic skills: giving one direction at a time, prompting the students to turn and look at you, mobilizing students movement, and using your voice command mode. These underlying principles are the most critical elements to consistent success. Direction techniques are used to increase effectiveness, understanding, and follow through, in lesson instruction. They are also used to mobilize students for organized activities, engagers, and classroom routines or rituals, including cleaning up, putting away books and materials, and lining up for lunch or recess.

Your directions must be clear and concise—this makes perfect sense, right? Let me see if I can create a visual for you. You are in the audience and you watch me raise my hand as I say "Raise this hand." Now the quandary happens: you think *Do I raise the hand on the left or right side of the room?* This is ambiguity. Ambiguity leads to uncertainty, and uncertainty leads to threat. If there is a chance your students will get something wrong in front of their classmates, they're not going to do it.

**AMBIGUITY LEADS TO UNCERTAINTY,** AND UNCERTAINTY LEADS TO **THREAT.**

Have you seen this next situation in a

large group? The instructor tells everyone in the room to turn to the right and shake their partner's hand. What's the problem? When everyone turns to the right, the person to your right as also turned to the right. *Ambiguity* again. Here's the dangerous part: as the learner, I think that you must not have meant for me to shake just one person's hand; you must have meant to shake the person's hand on both sides of me. This is the precarious moment when the instructor taught their learners, "I am going to give you a direction that makes no sense, so you can do what you think you should do."

When you give effective directions, not only are you building your credibility, but you are also building your learners' confidence in you.

**One Direction at a Time**

How many directions can students remember? Some teachers assert that even young classrooms can easily manage four or five directions. However, where possible, teachers will achieve the maximum level of success with directions if they give *one direction at a time.*

Teachers often talk too much. They over-explain concepts, repeat directions, and lengthen answers in a way that dilutes the impact of what they say.

As a teacher, you must learn to practice the personal discipline of giving one direction at a time. For instance, let's say you instruct students to get into a group, choose a leader, choose the writer, choose the speaker, and choose the materials manager. What was the first thing you instructed the students to do? First, they have to decide if it's a good group. They are asking themselves, "Who do I like in here?" or "Who likes me?"

Meanwhile, you've given two or three more directions and your students are all in their heads completing their social negotiation. What are they missing? That's right! The rest of the directions! When you discipline yourself to give one direction at a time, your students can get on task quickly and easily. Most of your learners want to be successful and follow your directions.

GET INTO GROUPS.....BLAH BLAH BLABH ... THEN GO AND.....BLAH BLAH BLAH....BLAH BLAH... AFTER THAT....BLAH BLAH... **Go!**

When you give a direction, what is the very next thing you have to do? Yep: wait for the students to accomplish what you have asked them to do. Unfortunately, teachers have developed a bad habit, albeit one we come by honestly. Because experience has taught us that there are several interruptions in any given class period, we fall into the pattern of giving as many directions as possible to get high-performing students dialed in to the task. Then we can help and coach students who seem to need more support. However, almost all this lost time can be recovered by giving one direction at a time.

Directions given one at a time are instrumental in making students feel confident they know what is going on and what is expected of them. Written directions are helpful as a guide when there are a lot of details to complete. Many learners may have difficulty understanding or remembering multiple-step instructions, especially if they are only verbal. Giving students several points related to the task leaves them confused or frustrated. Again, if a student thinks they are going to get something wrong in front of their peers, they're usually not going to participate or offer answers.

Refrain from lengthy descriptions. When instruction lasts longer than thirty to sixty seconds, students become listless because they can't remember all the input. Diction, enunciation, and speaking with a slower pace add to the learner's ability to comprehend directions and explanations. Solicit feedback from students on your direction pacing and adjust accordingly.[17]

### See Me and Cue Words

Imagine you've mastered giving one direction at a time and you decide it's time for group work. You've given your direction to get into a group and waited successfully for students to settle into their groups. With your groups seated in a circle, you begin to give them the information they need to start working. But there's a problem. If they are all seated in a circle, some students have their backs to you.

Another not-so-common commonsense notion is that teachers can maximize the effect of their directions if they remember that the majority of students prefer to *see* them when they give instructions.

If students do not have a clear line of sight, it is critical to take the time and have them adjust their bodies so that they can watch you from a comfortable position while maintaining their focus. When students are comfortable, they can better give their full attention—at least at the start of the directions. Then it is up to you to keep it!

I work with adults in settings including university, teambuilding, and leadership. If I do not tell them to sit so they can see me comfortably, they will stand or sit with their backs to me, mostly because they are trying to be respectful while still following my directions.

Why don't students just turn in their chairs so that they can see you? Because they are trying to do what you told them: get into a group and sit in a circle. Do you ever see them twist their backs so that they can lean over the back of their chairs to see you? The second big part of giving directions is telling them to turn so they can see you. Cooperation and follow-through on your instructions are more successful. Once you have given all the instructions for the group work, it is easy to give one direction to turn back to face the group to begin.

### Pairing a Visual Cue with a Verbal Command (Mobilization)

In most learning situations where the teacher is giving directions while facing students, it may be useful to pair a verbal direction with a visual cue. Use a visual cue such as pointing with an open hand in the direction in which you want to your student to mobilize.

Pairing a visual cue with a command is one of those finer points of efficiency when giving directions. Say you want the class to line up on the west side of the room or into the right corner of the room. Students do not always have a working sense of the cardinal directions such as east, west, north, south, clockwise, counterclockwise, or even left or right (port/starboard). They can easily figure it out with a bit of delay or simply following the group. The key phrase is delay.

If you are teaching directions such as left or right, then that is the lesson. If you want to quickly mobilize students, support your directions with a visual cue for efficiency. An example may look like this: ask the students to stand up, now that they are facing you. Tell the students to turn to their left. Watch their facial expressions and or gestures as they negotiate the instruction. Now instruct the group to turn back to the front of the room, and tell them to make one full circle clockwise. When I do this in a group I usually have one or two people wait to turn to their left and look to see which way the group is moving. Some students will use their fingers in an L shape to indicate to them which direction they should turn. Some will turn the opposite way and quickly correct as soon as they notice what the rest of the group is doing.

Additionally, mobilization could mean that the teacher chooses objects that are readily visible to everyone and incorporates them into the directions. If the room has an exit sign, the teacher can point to it while instructing students to gather under the sign.

### Command Mode And Congruency In Giving Directions

Great speakers throughout world history all share one critical characteristic—their ability to communicate a single message with power, conviction, and passion. The key is that *every aspect of the delivery* communicates the same message. Their choice of words, tone of voice, pacing, use of pauses, gaze, and physical gestures were all focused on a key idea. The term used to describe this effect is *congruence*. High levels of congruence generate a strong impact on students.

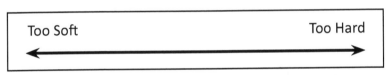

Command mode is an assertive form of giving directions. Imagine there is a continuum: one end is too soft and the opposite end is too hard.

When giving a direction in a too-soft manner, it is as if you're begging students to comply. A passive directive hopes to make all students happy. This pleasing-the-learners approach implies you are trying to avoid conflict or ask students to like you. It is also a potential catastrophe when students go off-task—and they will go off-task. If you let it slide until you can't take it anymore, frustration usually creeps in and you growl at the learners.

If you are giving directions on the opposite end of the continuum, you may come off as a loud drill sergeant. This over-directive approach is too aggressive. It sets you up to use the words "always" and "never," making students feel as if they are bad people who never do anything right. This directive format results in alienation rather than respect.

This is where <u>command mode</u> fits in on the continuum; it is just on the inside of being too hard.

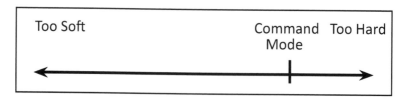

Command mode is an assertive manner of giving directions. It is a straightforward, no-nonsense approach. You do not beg, plead, or threaten. Instead, you use a forthright approach that communicates your expectation—I'm not asking you, I'm telling you. This is where you pull from the life experience of veteran teachers. They have learned how to be assertive from years of managing classes.

Now let's add congruence to our directions. Posture is both a practice and a subject. When you are congruent in giving directions, everything you do—your body posture, your eyes, your hands, even your feet—communicates to students. Let's say you give a command to stand up. Your body language is saying stand up. Your gaze is strong, your hands are up in the air, and you are standing still. Everything you communicate models what you want the learners to do. It is as if you are willing them to stand up. This is being congruent. Say what needs to be said with the greatest amount of clarity and the least amount of words. It's economy of language.

## The Four-Part Sequence

A particular sequence of phrases can provide an effective organization of information for students. Below is a four-part sequence based on natural language patterns developed by Rich Allen. Always tell the students the "when" before the "what." Students must listen all the way through since the keyword is not given until all the directions have been given.[18]

### Four-part sequence for giving directions

1. **Primer.** Holding place for students…[examples might be] "In ten seconds…" "In a moment…" " In thirty seconds…" (Place a time frame to the beginning of the direction)

2. **Release Word /Prompt** [examples might be] "When I say go…" "When I say blue…" "When I say tsunami…" (Add a prompt word to indicate when the action will begin)

3. **State the direction:** Get to the point. Begin direction-giving statements with an action verb: [examples might be] "Move the chairs to the sides of the room…" "Take," "Write," "Talk," "Draw," "Move."

4. **Say the Release Word.** "Go!" "Blue!" "Tsunami!" (Say the embedded release word to initiate the action)

Use few words in a clean and clear-cut manner. Use cue words quickly and efficiently. This four-part sequence is a series of cues that call the learner's attention and guide the learners quickly.[19] Work to eliminate unneeded words and phrases and say only what is necessary. For example, stop using phrases such as "I want you to..."or "What I'd like you to do is..." or "You're going to..." These added phrases muddle the direction and confuse the listener. Due to the lengthy description of what students are going to do, they usually immediately ask, "What are we supposed to do?" This four-part structure is designed to condition learners to take notice that a direction is coming. They need to listen for it and respond accordingly, efficiently, and in a timely way.

## Complex Directions

The art of giving effective directions is routinely underappreciated.

---

### First: (Why) *Overall Frame*

The frame tells the group 'why' they will be participating in this activity. You need to answer what's in it for them. Framing is further explained in Chapter 4.

### Second: (What) *Big Idea*

This is the objective, the *big idea* of what the students are going to do. This also gives students a plan or structure to hold on to while the rest of the details are being described.

### Third: (How To) *Basics*

The *basics* of the activity, the "how to" complete the project or challenge.

### Fourth (Little How To's) *Details*

These are the *details* and the specifics within the activity.

### Fifth (Answer Questions)

This is where you open up the discussion to answer questions related to the student's success for the project or activity.

---

Figure 4: Complex Directions Model

The choice of the word *art* in this phrase is deliberate. Effective directions are truly an art form unto themselves. They require the artist's gift of personal expression, built on a strong foundation of technical expertise. The teacher seeking to ensure maximum efficiency when giving directions must follow the same path as the beginning artist. Mastery of the underlying principles of giving effective directions is the most critical element to consistent success.

When you need to give a set of directions for a complex activity, use this model to help with the intricacies of the project. Always start by answering the "why."

### *Some Final Tips for giving effective directions*
- Use expression and body language to enhance understanding
    - Gestures and body language (hand signal, physical expression) add context for making the message clear. Note of caution: not all gestures carry the same cultural meanings. Check out culturally considerate gestures with resident experts
- Speak slowly and clearly with diction; enunciate clearly
- Be natural without overdoing it or sounding condescending
- Progressively increase your rate to match the students' level of proficiency
- Use shorter sentences with simpler syntax
- Use pause effect between phrases, for visuals, and during instruction to increase students' comprehension and retention of academic comprehension
- Demonstrate authentic respect for students and their cultures by using a friendly, approving approach
- Motivate and reduce the threat in the classroom through engagers and opportunities to be successful socially in order to

increase risk-taking and participation

- Promote a "can-do" and *success* atmosphere in all encounters
- Maintain warm, authentic, supportive AFFECT

### Closing Thoughts

We use state changes to keep our students in a refreshed and optimal learning state. Your timing comes from reading the energy of the students and the crest of the wave. Using music will become a favorite with you and your learners alike.

Sharpen your discipline to give only one direction at a time. The art comes when the orchestration of all the direction-giving components becomes automatic. The more you instruct the students to see you, master your command mode, and use the four-part sequence, the more you will reap the benefits that come with keeping learning fresh, novel, interesting, and masterfully managed.

As you refine your timing with the flow of instructional methods, state changes, use of music, and direction-giving skills, your instructional delivery will rise to an exceptionally successful, interactive level of teaching. This is just the beginning of adopting an engaging practices mindset. Now we look at what we can do to turn up the climate in our classrooms.

# Turn It Up!
# Climate Control

Everything speaks! Everything in the environment sends a message that either enhances or detracts from learning. Your classroom environment and atmosphere represent your expectations. In setting the tone for your content, you use engagers to support student participation and create a climate of contagious energy for learning.

Climate control not only refers to the physical aspects of the classroom, but the atmospheric conditions that create a friendly *user space,* the elements of conscientious attention. Our environment has an effect on our brains. We enrich our learning environment by creating a space that promotes approachability and receptiveness. Pay attention to eye-catching details and provide a clean, warm, and organized learning environment. Even the writing on whiteboards when demonstrating a lesson component sends a message to our learners about the type of work we expect in return.

Many times, paying attention to our classroom climate tends to be more of a behind-the-scenes attention to details. We influence the atmosphere from the way we organize our chairs and desks to the visual aesthetics of the words and posters we put on our walls. Appearance is a huge factor in securing students' respect for the learning environment. Our elementary colleagues are probably the best at setting up the room walls and space to support student learning. We tend to become content specialists at the middle school, high school, and tertiary levels, and we sometimes overlook our climate.

I once witnessed a student body change its destructive nature after the staff completely updated the student center with new paint, posters, and repaired tables and chairs. Previously, we replaced drywall regularly from students punching the walls or throwing chairs. After we made some simple upgrades, we noticed a change in regard for the space. The students' affect changed significantly, and they showed pride in their student center. What are some cool environmental enhancements that you can make to your own classroom. See Figure 5.

| Refreshing environments: Upgrade your physical space by giving your environment a fresh look. | | |
|---|---|---|
| Fresh paint | Fresh air | Books and magazines |
| Clean aromas | Comfortable furniture | Stuffed animals |
| Living plant(s) | Flowers or plant on the | Sunny room |
| Attractive, up-to-date bulletin boards | desk | Matching colors |
| | Open doors | Positively-worded signs |
| | Candy jar with candy | Bright hallways |
| Soft lighting | Soft music | Clean windows |
| Big and soft pillows | Attractive pictures | Clear floors |
| Lots of books | Comfortable temperature | |

Figure 5: Refreshing Environments

# ENVIRONMENT

Our physical environments influence how we feel, hear, and see. Purposeful comments, behaviors, and positively-worded posters support an upbeat and responsive environment. We can regulate the tone and impression of a physical space with a well-presented visual, plants, books, desk and chair arrangement, natural lighting, and use of technology. The atmosphere is enhanced by signage on the walls, cleanliness, organization, and acknowledgment walls featuring student pictures, good work, and positive feedback. A picture is worth more than a thousand words. When you use a visual in a learning situation, something fascinating happens. These connections strengthen initial learning by stimulating the visual reaction and provide a rich context for new learning. Add content posters to prime your learners for new content and reinforce concepts they have learned recently. Hang them high on the walls so your students access their visual cortex by looking up to see them.

As the level of education climbs, so does the sophistication level of personal and acknowledgment walls. Better awareness, smarter planning, and simple changes can improve learning in every classroom environment.

Where students sit in a room impacts their cognition and stress levels. Seating can affect student success in several ways. Students care about who they sit next to, a friend or foe, and whether they sit up front next to the teacher or safely positioned in the third or fourth row. How student seating is arranged can foster important social and peer interaction. Behavior issues advise our seating decisions as well.

Research suggests that students have better concentration sitting in rows; however, rows are not always best for collaborative learning or group work. One study found that students seated in a semi-circle rather than rows tended to ask more questions.[20] Earlier studies show the benefit of cluster seating for group discussions and interactive learning tasks. The key here is to match the seating arrangement to the activity. Use cluster arrangements for group and collaboration and row seating when concentrated independent learning is your goal. Environments do matter; we do what we can with what we have.

$$B=f\,(PE)$$

Behavior is a function of both the person and the environment

Lewin (1936)

# ATMOSPHERE

Environment and atmosphere are interconnected and overlap in many ways. They should complement each other. While environment refers to the physical look, design, and organization of a classroom, atmosphere refers to the feeling and emotion emanating in the classroom. Inviting comments, approachable behaviors, and appealing signs help to elicit a warm and safe atmosphere. (See Figure 6) What we do and how we show up as a teacher influences the atmosphere as much as the classroom environment. Check out the list of inviting comments, approachable behaviors, and appealing signs in Figure 5 below. Like the positive aspects we work to support in our environments, we also have negative and neglected spaces with equal influencing power. Tap into your creative colleagues for help and ideas. You will improve your students' attitude ever so slightly with more respect and gratitude for a well-organized, clean, and thought-out classroom climate. Create a student-friendly environment by making your class setting convey the feeling that you are interested in them and care about them. Watch their personal connections flourish and personal strength grow.

Research suggests that if you create a warm and caring environment, attendance and student performance will increase. Create a photo board with class pictures taken throughout the term. Have games and puzzles for the age group you teach to experiment with while waiting for class to start. Add some color or pictures to your room. Create a suggestion box for ways to make the classroom better. Add an acknowledgment wall. Show the love!

Like the positive aspects we work to support in our environments, we also have negative and neglected spaces with equal influencing power. Tap into your creative colleagues for help and ideas.

**Inviting comments: Use these comments to promote a welcoming climate.**

| | | |
|---|---|---|
| Good morning. | I enjoy having you here. | Welcome. |
| Let's talk it over. | I understand. | That's even better. |
| How can I help? | We missed you. | I've been thinking of you. |
| Tell me about it. | I'm glad you came by. | How are things going? |
| I appreciate your help. | I like that idea! | I'd like your opinion. |
| Of course I have the time. | Please come in. | What do you think? |
| You made me feel good. | I think you can do it. | May I help you? |
| | Please tell me more. | Let's do it together. |
| | | I enjoy our time together. |

**Approachable behaviors: These behaviors increase your receptiveness.**

| | | |
|---|---|---|
| A relaxed posture | Sharing lunch together | Giving wait-time |
| Smiling | Being on time | Yielding interest |
| Listening carefully | Sending a thoughtful note | Learning names |
| Opening or holding a | Bringing a gift | Offering refreshments |
| door for someone | Sharing an experience | Sharing a poem |
| Giving a friendly wink | Extending a hand | Expressing regret |
| Giving a thumbs-up | Remembering important | Overlooking a faux pas |
| sign | occasions | |
| Offering someone a | | |
| chair | | |

**Appealing Signs: Use positively-worded signs that reinforce a learner friendly environment.**

| | | |
|---|---|---|
| Welcome | Have Lunch with | Open House |
| Open, Come in | Welcome Back Students | No Appointment |
| Please Use Other Door | Please Excuse the | Necessary |
| Come Back Soon | Inconvenience | Come on In |
| We're Glad You're Here | Please Touch | Visitor Parking |
| Sorry I Missed You, | May We Help You? | Please Use Sidewalks |
| Please Come Back | I'll Be Back at _____ | Please Leave Message |
| Please Place Trash | Please Watch Your Step | |
| Here | Help Us Conserve Energy | |
| Come As You Are | Directory Assistance | |

Figure 6: Atmosphere Enrichment

| Unpleasant Environments | Antagonistic Signs |
|---|---|
| Dark corridors | Do Not Disturb |
| Bad smells | No Talking |
| Dingy colors | No Running in Halls |
| Full trash cans | No Admission without Pass |
| Hard lighting | Office Closed |
| Dirty coffee cups | Visitors Must Report to: |
| Bare or burned-out light bulb | No Admittance |
| Stack of out-of-date materials | Be Seated |
| Fluorescent lights that buzz | Keep Out |
| A full pencil sharpener | Do Not Enter |
| Dead plant | No Deposit, No Return |
| Dingy curtains | By Appointment Only |
| Opaque windows | Out of Order |
| Cold room | We Do Not Give Change |
| Artificial plants and flowers | Do Not Enter |
| Straight rows | Take a Number and Wait |
| Peeling paint and plaster | Keep This Door **Shut**! |
| Nothing to read | Do Not Remove Under Any |
| Dusty, cobwebby shelves | Circumstance! |
| Stuffy room | |
| Sticky or dirty floors | |
| Signs with letters missing | |

Figure 7: Contributors to a Negative Atmosphere

WHEN TENSION GOES UP,

# RETENTION

GOES DOWN

Engaging Practices:
How to Activate Student Learning

# TURNING UP THE CLIMATE BY USING ENGAGERS

We can show students how to apply content through small group exercises, games, case studies, brainteasers, and roleplay. We call these engagers. When we facilitate engagers in our classes regularly, we help our students practice academic as well as social skills. We can and want to use engagers to stimulate learners into a positive state for continued learning. When we use engager activities with our students, we create opportunities that empower friendships. Where the attention goes, the energy flows.

The custom of using engagers refreshes and energizes students into a receptive learning state along with endorsing personal presence. Oftentimes students enter the classroom with distracted minds. The use of a quick engager helps them focus and pay attention in the moment. Engagers are playful in nature, but can serve as brainteasers or cognitive puzzles as well. Review examples of engagers in the appendix that instill energy and laughter opportunities for your learners. Use engagers as needed, either throughout the day or a minimum of three to four per week. They can be adapted to relate to content or simply used reenergize a group. In addition, engagers can often redirect potential behavioral disruptions.

**Fifteen Ways Engagers can REDUCE Problem Behaviors**

1. Taking part in an engager can reduce the potential for boredom and behavioral acting-out interruptions.
2. Students might see a mixture of "work" and "play" as a fair pact and be more willing to work when play is part of the deal.
3. Engagers can help develop relationships with peers. Better relationships, in turn, increase the range and quality of academics.

4. Engagers can assist group functioning and development, which in turn can improve the quality of group discussions.

5. Doing engagers with police officers, resource officers, or other authority figures can grow positive connections and improve attitudes all around.

6. Engagers provide more opportunities for positive interactions and can surprise teachers with insight about a student's capabilities and good nature.

7. An experience of success with engagers helps develop self-esteem. This can deter offending behavior in which low self-esteem is a contributory factor.

8. Positively experienced engagers can become a substitute for the esteem needs that were previously met through misbehavior.

9. Age appropriate engagers provide students a positive experience in and of itself.

10. Reviewing negative experiences that arise during engagers can provide useful insights into difficulties related to misbehavior.

11. When learners are involved and have ownership in the organization and design of engagers, they become more capable of influencing events around them.

12. Engagers give students the social opportunity to benefit from the process of making things happen and to see the results of their efforts.

13. Engagers can be set up as skill training exercises. Improving skills in decision-making, problem-solving, planning, assertiveness, or self-control reduces the chances of further misbehavior.

14. Teachers can loosen personal constructs or stretch their personal paradigms to awaken students' sense of freedom and curiosity, which makes them more open to learning.

15. Using engagers can be used as a way for values clarification and character development

Remember when using engagers that the art of effective directions can have direct impact on the success of your use of an engager. We use engagers to turn up our climate and develop guided social growth opportunities for learners. Using one direction at a time is much easier with a state change or an activity that doesn't require many steps. An engager or a game activity, on the other hand, can be more complex. Use the following guide as simple cueing. Most engagers only take five to seven minutes, time well spent in many respects. We reenergize the group, provide social growth opportunities, support group development, and decrease possible behavioral disruptions.

## Elements of Effective Engager and Game Set-Up

You may refer to the complex directions model (in Chapter 1).

- Remember clarity of directions—use few words, and give only one at a time
- Use directions to mobilize—stance, tone, use of body movements to model placement of students
- Read the room—as everything progresses, go with the flow, redirect the flow, as needed
- Reinforce emotional safety issues— decrease vulnerability and increase risk taking
- Be honest and open—work to build in curiosity thorough novel invitation
- Be creative—make the game fresh and interesting by using characters to assign roles (i.e, Batman & Robin, Peanut butter & Jelly)
- Use your own style—let your personality carry the enthusiasm
- Be fun and light—enjoy yourself, being strict is a spirit killer; keep participation light-hearted. Sometimes our need to control gets in the way of teaching

- Use the 4 Part Sequence—"When I say go…"
- Get to the point; begin direction-giving statements with an action verb:
  - Take
  - Write
  - Talk
  - Draw
  - Move

HOT TIP—say what needs to be said with the greatest amount of clarity and the least amount of words. It's economy of language.

## MUSIC AS A COMPONENT OF YOUR CLIMATE AND ATMOSPHERE

Music boosts the climate and atmosphere powerfully and effortlessly. The climate is influenced or hindered by music as well. Music conveys emotional information. We're not talking about lyrics here, but melody and other aural aspects of music. Use music in the classroom to:

- Create a desired atmosphere
- Build a sense of anticipation
- Energize learning activities
- Focus concentration
- Increase attention
- Improve memory
- Facilitate a multi-sensory learning experience
- Release tension
- Enhance imagination
- Align groups
- Develop rapport

**WHERE WORDS FAIL...**
**MUSIC SPEAKS**

- Provide inspiration and motivation
- Add an element of fun
- Accentuate theme-oriented units

Talk about engaging practices—music delivers immediate results!

## Four Standard Places to Use Music in the Classroom

We use music to move people from one location to another and create the atmosphere of a desired learning state. We anchor specific activities to a song and provide an emotional link through lyrics to relax or energize. Preparing for a learning experience can make a difference between lessons that engage learners and lessons that just pass the time. Certain music will create a positive learning atmosphere and encourage students to feel comfortable to participate. In this way it also has great effect upon students' attitudes and motivation to learn. The four places you may use music are at the start of class, during movement, as background during discussion, and at the end of class.

### 1. Pre-class welcoming music: Use upbeat music that sets the tone for the day

First of all, let's define the first three minutes of class. To me, class begins for a student as soon as he or she walks through my classroom door. In essence, this is your opportunity to set the tone for class and create a positive learning atmosphere. Your classroom environment begins affecting students immediately upon their entrance. If you are planning on doing some activities at the beginning of class, then upbeat music will add energy to the group. If your lesson is contemplative or emotionally challenging and requires a quieter setting, you might use some softer classical or instrumental music to set that tone.

## 2. During movement: Fast music with a strong beat for increased blood flow

Whenever your lesson calls for movement such as rearranging chairs and desks to do an activity, you should take the opportunity to play faster-paced music. Music provides a positive environment that enhances student interaction and helps develop a sense of community and cooperation. If you have never done this before, you will be amazed to observe the difference in your students' energy level while the music is playing.

Use upbeat, popular music during transitions or movement activities to increase productivity or energize students during daily energy lulls. Use music that inspires you to move or something you may hear in an exercise class. Generally, this music has 125-145 beats per minute (BPM). I avoid techno (too fast), explicit lyrics, and heavy rap, mostly due to the profanity. But hip hop tends to have an "up" beat, which creates a positive effect in the classroom.

If you are new at using music in your classrooms, finding appropriate music can be a bit challenging. Your students are a great resource for types of popular music to choose. Be sure to check if the music is labeled "explicit" on the source you are using. iTunes, Spotify, and Pandora label their music as explicit if the lyrics contain profanity. In addition, I do not use explicit songs that were changed to "clean" lyrics. Even though I was playing a clean version of a song, I found that my students still sang explicit lyrics out loud. I was once embarrassed because I was being observed that day, and the students' renditions did not go over well with my lead instructor.

### 3. Background (discussion) music

Music acts as a "pad" during discussions or group activities, blocking out sounds from one group that might interfere with another group. Using soft music in the background increases attention level, relaxes the mind, improves retention and memory, extends focused learning time, and increases cognition.

Soft background music without words can help students remain focused and stay on task when working on an assignment or sitting quietly at their desks. Music is the doorway to the inner realms, and the use of music during creative and reflective times facilitates personal expression in writing, art, movement, and a multitude of projects. Calming music helps to relax the mind while students study, read, or write.

Well-selected background music boosts creativity and arousal. Research indicates the ideal music to increase cognition is repetitive, familiar, instrumental, and played at low-to-moderate volume.[21] Background music can stimulate internal processing, facilitate creativity, and encourage personal reflection. When students are writing or journaling, reflective music such as solo piano in either classical or contemporary styles holds their attention for longer periods of time. In one study, students wrote twice as much with music than without!

### 4. At the end of class: Celebration songs

Music at the end of class can leave students with a positive impression of the time that was just spent with you. Music has a powerful ability to impact the emotions we feel. Remember, the last thing you feel at the end of a class is often what stays with you. The next time a student thinks about your class, they will remember a positive feeling and associate learning with joy.

As you can see, there are many ways using music in your classrooms can enhance your engaging practices. Enjoy giving it a go!

**Closing Thoughts**

Our environment, the atmosphere we create, the design of our lesson delivery or educational tasks, use of engagers, including music, how we dress, the way we listen, and the character traits we model all send messages to our students. By being deliberate and proactive in the messages students receive, you better manage the variables that contribute to an optimal classroom atmosphere and learning environment.

# Social-Emotional Mindfulness

"A good head and a good heart are always a formidable combination." - Nelson Mandela

## POSITIVE PSYCHOLOGICAL CAPITAL AND RELATIONSHIPS

Where you start doesn't matter—it's where you end up. "Students may never remember what you taught them, but will never forget how you make them feel." This age-old saying is spot-on. The social-emotional assets component is the heart and soul of the engagement model I discuss in this book. Tapping into the hearts of our learners gives us a platform to aid students in growing positive psychological capital. This, in turn, affords us a forgiving teaching environment. The students care more about us and not so much about our ability to use state changes, our awesome creative style with using music, our fine craft to give effective directions, or our ability to turn up the climate. While those skills make your instruction impactful, it is your relationships and your ability to empower students with proactive social assets and positive psychological capital that fosters resilience.

GOOD THINGS HAPPEN **WHEN YOU MAKE** GOOD THINGS HAPPEN

### Social-Emotional Mindfulness

I'd like to make a case for not only the value, but also the need, to provide the necessary situations to grow social-emotional skills in our students. Your goal is to ready your students for the next level of complexity on a soft skills level. Your students' ability to manage stress, conflict, rejection, and failure gives them the skills to be successful in personal relationships and future work or career choices.

Helping your students successfully negotiate daily social demands is a challenge that faces every teacher every day. When you provide your learners with powerful social-emotional skill opportunities, you empower their personal navigational abilities to manage and bounce back from betrayal, loss, and disappointment. We end up giving students communication skills that help them self-advocate for respect by friends, future bosses, and future significant others.

Offering opportunities to develop social-emotional soft skills is just as critical as any other part of education. Research supports the value of engaging appropriate emotions. They are an integral and invaluable part of every student's educational experience. Social contact has significant and broad-based effects. Because our students spend so many hours of their lives in school, we must consider what we're doing to their social-emotional development during this time. Socially, we are influencing them a great deal. If you believe that school is about the "whole person," the social-emotional side is worth understanding and addressing.

The Collaborative for Academic, Social, and Emotional Learning (CASEL)[22] defines social-emotional learning as the process through which children and adults acquire and effectively apply the knowledge, attitudes, and skills necessary to understand and manage emotions, set and achieve positive goals, feel and show empathy for others, establish and maintain positive relationships, and make responsible decisions.

At its basic level, learning is social. If a student fails at recruiting assistance or jointly participating in activities, learning will suffer. Social development is at the heart of intellectual, emotional, and physical development.

What stops students from moving forward, taking action or being their best? What controls and determines the quality of their lives? The answer is *fear*. Fear can destroy our psychology and immobilize us from taking action. All of us experience fear in some context during our lives; fear of rejection, fear of failure, fear of success (handling the pressure to deliver at a high level), fear of love (or losing love), fear of being alone, or fear of the unknown. In fact, most of us feel a combination of these fears over the course of our lives. How might a youth be managing these emotions? Fear is hardwired into every human being—the secret is in learning how to use fear instead of letting fear use you! Focus equals feeling, real or perceived. We believe what we focus on.

Two primary fears we share as human beings:

1. We are not enough.
2. We won't be loved—rejection.

Researchers Eisenberger, et.al.[23] have found a physiological basis for social pain by monitoring the brains of people who thought they had been maliciously excluded from a computer game by other players. The study supported a strong association in our need for social connection. There's something about exclusion from others that is perceived as being as harmful, as something that can physically hurt us, and our body responds accordingly.

Eisenberger and her co-authors created a computer game in which test subjects were led to believe they were playing ball with two other players. At some point, the other players seemed to exclude the test subject from the game, making it appear the test subject had been suddenly rejected and blocked from playing with the group.

The distress of this rejection registered in the same part of the brain for all players, the anterior cingulate cortex (ACC). The ACC is the same part of the brain that is associated with physical pain.

"Throughout history poets have written about the pain of a broken heart," Jaak Panksepp of the Department of Psychology at Bowling Green State University in Ohio said in a commentary in the journal *Science*.[24] It seems that such poetic insights into the human condition are now supported by neurophysiological findings.

The tendency to feel rejection as an acute pain suggests that the need to be accepted as part of a social group is as important to humans as avoidance of pain. Our need to develop connections with and among our students has significant behavioral implications. It is a basic function of the human experience to feel soothed in the presence of closeness to others and to feel distressed when left behind.

By attending to and knowing the social needs of your classes, you may be able to determine behavioral disruptions sooner and intervene swiftly and compassionately, as if a student had just fallen and hurt themselves.

What you appreciate, appreciates. As we create relationships of "enough," we promote social and emotional support.

In many ways, human connection is predictable. As we connect with our students, we create give-and-take in relationships. We typically connect with others when we:

**...Feel Liked.** The quality of likeability includes warming our smile with our eyes. When we are seen as likable, we are able to convey empathy, compassion, and caring.

**...Feel Empowered.** We empower our students and ourselves when we offer overt and subtle opportunities to have ownership in the classroom.

**...Feel Trust.** To be trusted, we need to be dependable. When we default to "yes," we can help the right things happen to create safety zones that help our students take healthy risks. We also need to feel trust for our students—often before they are willing to completely trust us.

**...Feel Accepted.** As adults, we need to be unassuming, open, and approachable. We create an atmosphere that offers a level playing field, allowing students to find their own power. This efficacy often displays its true colors in the students being vulnerable with us.

**...Feel Alive.** We ignite learners' minds and passions so they are invested and curious. This sort of excitement makes us feel alive.

There is enough for everyone, everywhere to have a happy, healthy, productive life. Developing social skills is a task commonly found in elementary schools, but the practice is somewhat neglected in middle school, high school, and the tertiary levels because our objectives are content delivery. Our ability to foster social-emotional (soft skill) development leads to healthy, resilient, and productive lives. When we blend social opportunity into our curriculum, we get significant payoff in terms of efficiency, fewer disruptions, better friendships, and

increased satisfaction with learning at all levels. Too little cooperation leads to social isolation. The negative effect of social isolation puts our students at risk of negative behaviors resulting in behavioral outbursts.

As we construct a supportive environment with compelling biases that promote social-emotional development, we grow positive psychological capital, which research is showing provides positive gains in hope, efficacy, resiliency, and optimism.

### Positive Psychological Capital

Psychological Capital (PsyCap) is a meta concept that incorporates various traits that have been found to foster psychological resilience. An individual's positive psychological state of development is characterized by (1) having confidence *(efficacy)* to take on and put in the necessary effort to succeed at challenging tasks; (2) making a positive attribution *(optimism)* about succeeding now and in the future; (3) persevering toward goals and, when necessary, adjusting routes to goals *(hope)* in order to succeed; and (4) when beset by problems and adversity, sustaining and bouncing back and even beyond *(resilience)* to attain success.[25]

Positive psychology literature shows that some individuals are unable to curb the psychological impact of stressors and they suffer physical and psychological health symptoms.[26] Other individuals have the capacity to rebound and experience little or no change in their capacity to function. According to Tugade and Fredrickson, these latter individuals demonstrate psychological resiliency;[27] that is, effective adaptation and coping in the face of adversity. Individuals who believe that they can do something about their stress have more positive psychological adaption than those who do not hold such beliefs.[28] These individuals have "positive" traits and abilities, including optimism, positive emotionality, hardiness, hope and ego resilience, that correlate to physical and psychological health.

In another study, Riolli, Savicki, and Richards[29] report PsyCap skills positively buffered the impact of stress so that the relationship between stress and negative outcomes was reduced. The implication for you includes a focus on aspects of psychological capital within academic content, since PsyCap helps students persevere in their studies in a psychologically and physically healthier manner. Research suggests that teaching our students to develop strategies that can improve their PsyCap dispositions will facilitate coping with stress exposures. To develop PsyCap in your classroom, you need to shift the emphasis away from what is wrong with people to what is right with people, focus on strength as opposed to weakness, be interested in resilience as opposed to vulnerability, and be concerned with enhancing and developing wellness, prosperity, and good life skills.

PsyCap skills are efficacy, hope, optimism and resiliency. Efficacy can be described as confidence. It's a feeling or belief in your ability to do something well or succeed at something. In addition, efficacy is the feeling of being certain that something will happen or that something is true. To encourage confidence in your students, help them to set and adjust clear, measurable and achievable goals.

Next in line is hope, wanting something to happen or be true. Hope is the feeling that what is wanted can be had or that events will turn out for the best. You can encourage hope by reassuring learners, giving them a feeling of support, and helping them to plan a way to succeed.

Third is optimism, a feeling or belief that good things will happen

CHAPTER 3

in the future, or a feeling or belief that what you hope for will happen. You encourage optimism by acknowledging, broadcasting, and celebrating learners' success along with the success of others.

Finally, resiliency is a positive way of coping with adversity or distress. It is defined as an ability to recover from stress, conflict, failure, change, or an increase in responsibility. You encourage resiliency by giving students resources, relationships, and emotional support that help them recuperate from stress, conflict, failure, or changes in responsibility.

### Efficacy

Let's start with eleven ways to raise efficacy.

The learning success spiral is a self-supporting system that starts with a belief we have about our abilities or ourselves. This affects our actions, which affect our results, which reinforce our beliefs. If we are going to positively affect students' low self-efficacy, we need to interrupt their belief system.

**THE LEARNING SPIRAL**

### Raising efficacy:

1. Use activities in which students already feel confident and review their experience.
2. Review positive experiences in ways that highlight what individual students contributed to their success.
3. Do an activity twice, highlighting relative successes on the second occasion.
4. Use the group to identify and support achievement of individual objectives.

5. Ensure that there is a sense of progression for each student.

6. Search out suitable opportunities for delegating and trusting. Give students *REAL* responsibilities for the organization or quality of the activity so they are not simply participants.

7. Use engagers in which early success is likely, and where there is a good chance of further success soon after.

8. Convert competitive games into cooperative or creative ones.

9. Use a variety of review techniques that give students plenty of scope for expressing positive experiences (see closure activities in the appendix).

10. Encourage adventurous engagers, especially those likely to generate experiences of self-control, taking risks, and achieving what seemed impossible.

11. As needed, reframe experiences that are seen as failures.

Students with high self-efficacy tend to keep it that way because they don't blame external factors for their failures and more importantly they take personal credit for their successes.

Students with low self-efficacy tend to keep it that way by blaming themselves for failures and not taking any personal credit for successes. They might attribute their success to luck or to someone else's actions. So despite their "success," their self-efficacy and motivation remain low which keeps them in a vicious cycle from which it is difficult to escape. Through experiencing success and taking credit for it, students begin to regain some sense of control.

### *Hope and Optimism*

Hope and a sense of self-worth work together. If our belief is that we are valuable, then the idea of life having meaning is more likely to be part of our thinking. Hope keeps our minds at ease, lowers stress, and improves physical health. To make progress, we need to be able to imagine better alternative realities, and we need to believe we can achieve them.

Our students develop self-esteem and optimism by experiencing success even in the face of challenges.[30] When our learners experience success, help them see how they contributed to it, and label those actions as strengths. For example, "You did well on your test." "You're a hard worker to have been so prepared!" We don't need to tell them something is great when it isn't, but giving them credit for their own accomplishments builds self-efficacy and contributes to optimism.

When your student faces failure or negative situations, validate their feelings, but ask questions that can cause them to see things as learning versus failure. This helps them process (rather than deny) their emotions, but gives the situation perspective. Acknowledge the feelings of your students and help them focus on successes they have already had. Help them to look at how things can go better in the future or under different circumstances. For example, "I see you feel disappointed in your score." "Maybe you're having an off day." "You usually do better, and I'm sure you will do better next time." "These things happen and we just get back up." Then get them involved in another activity or practice for future success.

Help your learners see that there is good and bad in situations. You can make a game of looking for the silver linings in seemingly negative situations unrelated to a specific incident of failure. That way, when students look for the silver lining in their personal failures, they will have had some practice.

There's an inherent danger of correcting your students' unacceptable behavior with negative labels. Students tend to live up or down to your expectations, so if you say, "So-and-so is our whiner," or "So-and-so is our shy one," what may have been a passing phase becomes a more permanent identity. Our students' development is also held back when people around them don't let them change or grow, such as labeling them a "troublemaker," "slow learner," or "failure." These negative labels are destructive, quite the opposite of your teaching intentions.

Students watch and see us as constant examples. The good news about this is that you can teach by doing. Practice optimistic thinking yourself. When you achieve success, don't downplay it with false modesty; give yourself credit for a job well done in front of students. When things go wrong, don't make it bigger than it is; put things in perspective. Your modeling is more powerful than you think.

Vicki Zakrzewski[31] with the Greater Good Science Center tells us to teach students that there's more than one way to reach a goal. Studies show that one of the greatest challenges for students with low hope is their inability to move past obstacles. They often lack key problem-solving skills, causing them give up quickly. One way to promote problem-solving is to teach students to visualize different ways to reach their goal when faced with obstacles. Talk them through some of their strategies.

Build in success stories. Experiencing success usually requires creative thinking to overcome barriers. Tell your students success stories and give them books that portray how others have succeeded or overcome adversity. Share stories of people who have overcome adversity to reach their goals. Research has demonstrated that hope can be cultivated to strengthen action and support thinking toward goal achievement. You are in a strategic position to make a difference in students' hope. You help students develop personal strategies that support persistence in the face of adversity. If one way doesn't work, try another. Start by helping students to seek several ways around a problem. If their default failure reason is based on perceived lack of talent, help them reject that negative thinking. Interrupt that mindset and help students identify who can help them.

Encourage the student to take a break and come back to the challenge with fresh eyes. Along with schoolwork goals, keep this notion in the recesses of your mind. Goals built on internal, personal standards are more energizing than those based on external standards (imposed by peers, parents, or teachers). We need students to have personal goals along with school goals.

> "One of the most common causes of failure is the habit of quitting when one is overtaken by temporary defeat."
> - Napoleon Hill

### Resiliency

The American Psychological Association reports that a combination of factors contribute to resilience. Many studies show that the primary factor in resilience is having caring and supportive relationships within and outside the family. Relationships that create love and trust and offer encouragement and reassurance help bolster a person's resilience. Beyond building relationships, resilience requires courage and persistence in the face of hardship. While this psychological factor is still being heavily researched, it doesn't hurt to develop our students' coping skills along with making connections and building relationships. The use of engagers, personal projects, and social-emotional learning activities can assist students to set up social networks to support them in their hour of need.

Relationships are the foundation of success and resilience. You can NOT over communicate. Learn to listen and help students learn to listen to the people they enjoy and respect. Remind them to spend time with these friends and family members to help them to get out of negative relationships with fear-based qualities, like possessiveness or insecurity. Help students focus on developing sustainable, supportive relationships based on kind-heartedness and authenticity.

Some of your students come to school with too much parental protection and don't know how to deal with failure, rejection, or disappointment. Others come to school having experienced too much hardship and don't have any willpower left to cope anymore. No matter the students' mindset or background, pay attention to despair, defeat, and loss in your students. You need to listen to their loss and help learners problem-solve for productive solutions for these feelings. Some of your students will bounce back quickly. You want to catch those who don't. Watch for their reactions to failure, emotional pain, and rejection— these are considered psychological wounds. You want to intervene and help students take action to overcome or constructively cope with social or emotional isolation.

The nature of a psychological wound is that one easily leads to another. To stop an emotional spiral, you need to teach self-compassion. Watch for negative thoughts and habitual rumination. Dr. Guy Winch suggests that you can interrupt self-disregard by engaging in tasks that take concentration.[32] Studies show that two minutes of distraction reduces the focus on unhealthy negativity. The same goes for building emotional resilience. Get into the habit of taking note about your students' psychological health on a regular basis, especially after stressful, difficult, or emotionally painful situations. Emotional awareness of your students takes a little time and effort, but it will seriously elevate their quality of life.

Guide students with time-management skills. Emphasize how to plan for unforeseen glitches and the demands of school responsibilities. Help students identify time conflicts and how to prepare for them. Underscore the need for rest and ways to reenergize themselves. Along with coordinating school demands with play, presence, and love of friends or significant others, you must help your students prioritize and balance school with life.

Here are a few options that help promote your students' resiliency management with the energy-depleting treadmill of worry, anxiety and fear:

1. Promote personal journal writing prompts for five minutes.
    - List any worries or anxieties…
    - Write a letter to someone about your concerns…(not to be delivered)
    - How would your favorite fictional character (Superman, Wonder Woman, or another hero) solve this issue?
    - Many more writing prompts can be found on the Internet.
2. Provide opportunities to practice being still in the classroom to help students relax their minds.
3. Help students identify what works best for them.
4. Provide opportunities to sit outdoors.
5. Play relaxing music.

Have students observe their worries, fears, and thoughts instead of being driven by them. Give them a metaphoric strategy such as a placing their worries in a "worry jar" as a way to rest the mind. Help students practice letting go for a while—they can pick up their worries again later.

Developing the PsyCap of your students, regardless of grade level, isn't only about academics or good grades. It's about preparing students with the soft skills it takes to get along with others easily, improving self-efficacy, hope, optimism, and increasing your students' resilience. More than academics, your students need to be equipped to manage the non-academic challenges of school. Now let's see what relationships have to do with this equation.

## RELATIONSHIPS REALLY DO MATTER

You have the capacity to be a true leader for positive change in your students. Using your skill set on how to connect makes a difference. To do so effortlessly, focus on how you can serve your learners. Furthermore, remember that influence happens in a moment, not in a long presentation. Be precise and specific as you guide students to reach your intended outcome. There are four primary tools we use to influence relationships.

### Tool #1: Create Massive Levels of Rapport

Rapport is connection. To create a long-term impact, you must show students that you care about them, you have their interests in mind, and that you like them. Use the invisible connection, allowing your beliefs and attitudes to transmit through your words, body language, and facial expressions. Ask yourself, "What do I respect about these students?" Make them feel significant. Allow your positive, sincere beliefs to be known. The brain responds favorably to care, sincerity, and unconditional accep-

tance. You don't get rapport by being nice. Tell students the truth in a non-judgmental fashion by connecting and caring so they feel like you like them. Embrace a service mindset and build rapport with humility, kindness, and authenticity.

**Check out these easy ways to create and build rapport:**
- Bring up a mutual interest.
- Make a startling statement.
- Tell a story.
- Listen.
- Pay a compliment.
- Give a gift.
- Have an incredibly intense belief: absolute emotional conviction.
- Learn to call your students by name.
- Learn something about your students' interests, hobbies, and aspirations.
- Know what students like, how they think, and how they feel about what's happening in their lives.
- Imagine what they say to themselves and about themselves.
- Know what keeps them from getting what they truly want. If you don't know, ask.
- Create and use personally-relevant class examples.
- Arrive to class early and stay late—and chat with your students.
- Explain your course policies, classroom rules, and why they are what they are.
- Post and keep office hours.
- Get online—use email to increase accessibility to your students.
- Interact more, lecture less—emphasize active learning.
- Reward student comments and questions with verbal praise.

- Be enthusiastic about teaching and passionate about your subject matter.
- Lighten up—crack a joke now and then.
- Be humble and, when appropriate, self-deprecating.
- Make eye contact with each student without staring, glaring, or flaring.
- Speak the truth to them in a way they can hear it clearly and gently.
- Remember to smile!

Have a sense of purpose. Your goal is to teach and support learning. Make sure this purpose is always fresh and present inside you. Break up your students' patterns of previous negative learning habits.

**Tool #2: Ask Questions**

Questions are your most powerful tool for building rapport with learners. When you understand what students believe and how they make decisions, all you have to do is show them that your teaching practices are consistent with those beliefs.

Guiding thoughts to help you:
- Find out what's really going on in students' heads.
- Find out their real motivations.
- Find out their beliefs.
- Take the pressure off.
- Ask questions that build rapport.
- Induce reciprocation.
- Put students in a reflective state.
- Bring out and overcome objections.

### Tool #3: Personal Congruency

Personal congruency means that your verbal and non-verbal communications match. Congruency comes from believing with conviction what you're saying and helps your students believe you. It's about how you act inside your classroom, and more importantly, how your behaviors align when you are outside your classroom. In many instances, it is the common saying of "walking your talk." Inside and outside the classroom, students will learn more from you by what they see you do than by what you tell them to do.

THE TEACHER AS A PERSON IS MORE IMPORTANT THAN THE TEACHER AS A TECHNICIAN. WHAT THEY ARE HAS MORE EFFECT THAN ANYTHING THEY DO

JACK CANFIELD

TODAY WE WILL LEARN ABOUT THE VALUE OF A HEALTHY DIET AND GOOD EXERCISE!

### Tool #4: Personal State Management

It's absolutely critical to manage your emotional state. If you let yourself get into a negative state like frustration, fear, or incompetence, you'll diminish your ability to maintain rapport. When we practice personal state management, we learn how to take negative states like rejection and behavior issues and turn them around so they empower rather than derail us.

Everything from our environment to our body language sends a message. Even the way we handle an incorrect response from a student in front of peers sends a message. Use this collection of powerfully present strategies to send that message to your learners' mindset, attitude, and belief systems.

***Have an incredibly intense belief: absolute emotional conviction.***
- Believe in your message; believe your students want to hear it.
- Care at the deepest level. See in your students more than they

currently see in themselves.

- Your *fallback* for anything you teach is integrity and caring. These are non-verbal cues that the students inherently feel from you.
- Break up your students' negative patterns.

### *Have a powerful physiology.*
- Fill the room with energy.
- The more you move (with purpose), the more you move students.
- Create variety and flow in your movement.
- Put yourself at a high energy level before you teach or present: be *present* with energy, intensity, and focus.

### *Know your outcome: the more clear and specific, the more powerful.*
- Begin with the end in mind.
- The unconscious mind will produce appropriate action if you keep reminding yourself of your outcome.
- Clarity is power.

### *Behavior flexibility.*
- The teacher with the most flexibility will always dominate, control, and shape the situation.
- Do the unexpected.
- Constantly change what you're doing.
- If something doesn't work, be willing to try something else: voice, body, tempo, or direction.
- Have a personal conflict model from which you operate.

### *Have fun: if it's not fun for you, it's not going to be fun for them.*
- Learners would rather be entertained than educated.

- The highest-paid people in our country are entertainers, not educators. Be an entertaining educator.

**WHAT WE LEARN WITH PLEASURE, WE NEVER FORGET.**

*Challenge your students: everyone wants to grow.*

- Students will respond if you are congruent, have rapport, and are teaching to serve them.
- Put yourself in a position where you get to raise their standard.
- Ask challenging questions—students respond to challenge.

*Energy: 80 percent of appeal is energy.*

- Pure physical energy is attractive in our culture.
- Use power, charisma, and charm.
- Make sure you have enough energy in your body before you even start. This is based on the way you eat, live and exercise.

"You absolutely must have fun. Without fun, there is no enthusiasm. Without enthusiasm, there is no energy. Without energy, there are only shades of gray." - Doug Hall

### Closing Thoughts

This is what we strive for as engaging, effective, influential teachers. Our ability to communicate, in combination with an effective learning design, provides a dynamic learning experience for all. Creating a positive, encouraging relationship is fundamental to your teaching role. To grow your students' social-emotional mindfulness strength is to grow your own.

Rapport gives back to your teaching in more ways than can really be measured. You need genuine connection to grow social-emotional mindfulness and psychological capital in your students.

We continually come to know our world and ourselves by making connections between the past, present, and future. Threads and themes help us to draw separate experiences together into stories about who we are. Introducing new social activity opportunities does not automatically lead to more hopeful and open-ended stories: young people may need help to make connections and learn from these experiences. Their world may need encouragement to change past prejudices and allow growth.

We all have a driving need to belong. Your students must establish their social group and define who likes them, who will support them, and who will care about them. As teachers, you need to understand and help them meet these needs.

We all want to be part of something big and exciting; we want to have purpose. As alive and engaged teachers, if you structure your content around social-emotional mindfulness, you create a trusting community that promotes risk-taking. As you engage through purposeful connection, your students become more engaged—and more engaged students make the time pass quickly for all involved. An engaged and active class also invites academic rigor. Your actions, thoughts and words can propel students beyond apathy, inspire their creativity, and increase their productivity.

# Linguistic Strategies: What You Say and How You Say It

There are a host of linguistic statements we use to position our content, promote curiosity, and support positive behaviors. These are called positioning statements. You use positioning statements to frame content so that students look forward to learning the information. In addition, you use a positioning statement to create interest or relevance. You can affect cooperation, improve inclusiveness, and impact behavior by getting specific about what students need to be doing.

You can turn learners on or off by how you choose to introduce anything, especially content. If you introduce your content by only stating the objective, it is often not enough to spark interest or invite students to want to know the information. If you have to say the objective first, follow it up with a positioning statement to "frame" and create buy-in. A frame is the 'why' of the lesson. It is so much more fun to teach to a group of interested and engaged learners. In this chapter, you will discover the effective use of frames, open loops, and the big three communication directives that promote amenability behavior: positive mental images, inclusion, and specificity.

Influential communication can be intentional and easy. With every interaction you have in the classroom, how you say things is just as important as what you say—maybe more important. Language and its structures require only that a teacher become aware of the effect of language when it is processed in the human mind. Those of us who want to be the most persuasive with our content must use our language insights to make the most reluctant learner interested and curious.

## CURIOSITY

Anticipation is typically a timing situation: often you know what you are going to do—it's a matter of how soon it happens. Curiosity is the state of wanting or waiting with positive expectancy; something left unanswered, unfinished or undone. It's a state of wanting to know the what, who, where, why and how of the lesson.

Curiosity correlates positively with intelligence. In one longitudinal study[33] researchers measured the degree of novelty-seeking behavior in 1,795 three-year-olds and then measured their cognitive ability at age eleven. As predicted, the eleven-year-olds who had been highly curious three-year-olds later scored twelve points higher on total IQ than low stimulation seekers.

In fact, in one of the largest undertakings in the field of psychology, two pioneers in the field of positive psychology, Martin Seligman, PhD, and Chris Peterson, PhD,[34] devised a scientific classification of the basic human strengths. This study identifies twenty-four basic strengths for authentic happiness; curiosity was one of five most highly associated with overall life fulfillment and happiness. Curiosity is the entry point to many of life's greatest sources of meaning and satisfaction: our interests, hobbies, and passions.

When you are curious about something, your mind expects and anticipates new ideas. When the ideas come, they will be quickly recognized. Without curiosity, the ideas may pass right in front of your learners, yet they miss them because their minds are not prepared to recognize them. You can create curious minds to look beneath the surface and discover new worlds of possibilities. The life of curious learners is neither dull nor routine. There are always new things that attract their attention; there are always new "toys" to play with. Instead of being bored, curious people have an adventurous life.

If you underestimate the power of using curiosity in your instruction, you'll be missing out on a huge influence tool that sets your students up for wanting more. You don't have to believe me now; the real amazement will be when you begin using this strategy with students.

This first linguistic strategy, "frames," I consider one of the most powerful tools in your teaching toolbox.

## FRAMES

Imagine I have a beautiful painting, but can't afford nice a frame. Does this influence your experience of the art? What if I add a beautiful, well-constructed frame; does that influence the way you see it? You bet it does! There are plenty of marketing studies to show that framed art will sell more quickly than art without a frame. So what am I talking about here? You can affect a learner's perception by using "frame" positioning statements that guide students to be interested.

The way you frame situations, interactions, and views of people affects their expectations, actions, decisions, and further perceptions. Framing theory suggests that how something is presented (the frame) influences the choices people make. Teachers can use framing with a profound effect on how students understand and respond to the world in which they live. It is a skill that most successful teachers possess, yet one that is not often taken advantage of.

While the principles of framing are easy to grasp, using frames requires pre-thinking and lots of practice. The way we act and what counts as a good or bad outcome directly relates to our language choices. A framing positioning statement is a tool to create an intentional bias. Productive framing leads to a positive climate, goal, and the engagement of actions. It can help us avoid apathy, confusion, or disinterest in the classroom.

Each learner enters the activity or content with his or her own mental frame. This frame influences the learning they take away from the experience. Each student may process the experience along an entirely different line of thinking. To ensure a more common outcome for learners, teachers may want to invest time in creating a common frame that will help guide students' thinking along the intended lines of instruction, encouraging them to listen and engage.

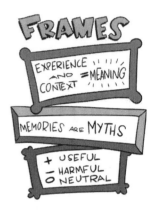

According to Fairhurst,[35] frames consist of three elements: Forethought, Thought and Language. Note context has been added to define framing content in classrooms.

1. Forethought:    Experience + Context = Meaning
2. Thought:    Memories Are Myths
3. Language:    Useful, Harmful, or Neutral

The <u>Forethought</u> element of frames is about Experience + Content = Meaning. I was raised to believe that we learn from our experiences.

There is one component, "context," that changes the experience. Take this example, a minor car accident where nobody was hurt. How might you describe it as a negative experience? Maybe it messed up your car, made you miss an appointment, was a huge inconvenience, or caused your insurance to go up. Now, how might you describe the accident as if it were a positive context? Maybe no one was hurt, I got a new paint job, I got to drive a new rental. You get it! The context is what changes our experience and creates meaning. It all boils down to perspective. When you carefully choose words for your frames in class, you can create a beneficial perspective for all students to listen to your content delivery.

Let's look at Thought; it is the idea that memories are myths. There is extensive research on the malleability of human memory. Elizabeth Loftus of the University of California, Irvine has published several works on memory and how our memories underserve us. Loftus is best known for her work on the misinformation effect and eyewitness memory. Courts of law have determined that eyewitness testimony can be the least reliable testimony, as it can be prejudiced by an investigator's interviewing techniques. Loftus's[36] findings illustrate that memory is highly flexible.

In another example, Loftus[37] conducted an experiment showing a group of 150 students a film of a car accident, followed by a series of questions. All questions were the same with exception of the last question. Half of the students were asked how fast was the car going when it "bumped" into the other car. The other half were asked how fast was the car going when it "smashed" into the other car. The group that thought the car "smashed" into the other car thought the car was traveling at a higher speed, than the car that "bumped" into the other car. Two words, 'bumped' and 'smashed', changed the memory of the students in the experiment. Memories are myths!

We use frame positioning statements to suggest another possible experience than what the student may bring to the learning. If you are working with a group of students who have failed to understand or be successful with previous content, they may have an unhelpful memory that could affect their outlook on your content. They need a frame that opens their mindset and helps them believe they can be successful. You want to tap into their need to know "what's in it for me?" also know as WIIFM in the active learning pedagogy. Frames help students approach your content with an open mind and interest.

Frame <u>Language</u> is rarely neutral. Imagine I had handed out an exam. Noticing the time, I tell my students, "Alright everyone, just two more minutes." What four-letter word is potentially harmful? "Just." What does that word imply? Rush, hurry, and panic. Is that the frame of mind you want for your students? It's hard to make that frame neutral or useful. To try and make it neutral, you can say, "Two minutes remain." To make a frame useful, you could say, "There's plenty of time; take this last two minutes to check your work and finalize your answers." Your aim here is to place the students in the most productive and calm mindset for finishing their work. If you can't frame it...don't teach it. You can help or hinder your students by the use of framing positioning statements in your language choices.

Frames are a part of what cognitive scientists call the "cognitive unconscious" structures in our mind. We know words through language. When we hear a word, its frame is activated in our mind. All of our previous experiences influence how we pay attention (or not) to the teacher. Changing the way learners see or hear content through careful language activates a mental frame. New language is required for new frames. Thinking differently requires speaking differently.[38,39]

Words signify meaning, but meanings can change based on how words are delivered. The simplest example is the use of rising inflection at the end of a sentence. "You're going to the store" can be a statement or a question depending on how the words are delivered. In print, you'd use a question mark to indicate you're posing a question, but in speech, meaning is conveyed solely through inflection.

**IF YOU CAN'T FRAME IT....DON'T TEACH IT**

The principle of purposeful word choice is to actively and intentionally use linguistics that enable students to be interested in the content, be receptive toward activities, and sometimes react more favorably around undesirable classroom chores like putting things away or cleaning up. The frame I use in this instance is, "Please help me 'zen' the room." Students would rather help me "zen" the room than clean the room. When I was teaching a Neuroscience and Teaching course at the university, I used this positioning frame to introduce a glossary and vocabulary exercise. "In order for us to really understand the workings of the brain, we need to be able to identify the brain structures, and more importantly, what these brain structures do." Then I promptly handed out index cards my students could use to create flash cards. That simple frame positioning statement created interest and purpose versus dread about vocabulary development. It set my students up to understand the need for, and have investment in, the activity.

Some students already approach learning with a defeatist attitude. You confirm their invisible fears or dreads when your frame is harmful or negative. Framing is about using language that fits your learners' worldview. It's not just language: ideas are primary, and language simply caries those ideas. To evoke those ideas, the basic premise of framing is to introduce content by avoiding defeating language.

Try this list of framing statements to generate interest, or at the very least, create a positive reaction:

- "For some of you this will be the most interesting information we will cover yet."
- "This is information we have been missing."
- "Some students said these next details were the most helpful."
- "This next section could be the most important information we cover this entire year."
- "In order for us to truly appreciate this next strategy, we need to…"
- "There were three elements we found during this analysis…"

**"The proper question is not, 'How can people motivate others?' but rather, 'How can people create the conditions within which others will motivate themselves?'"**
**- Edward Deci**

Doing something or learning something simply because we are told to is two-dimensional; it's flat learning. Understanding why the same information might be relevant, how it might connect to things we already know, creates a far more powerful multi-dimensional learning experience.

Framing will set you up for success. Start positioning your content with a well-thought out frame that creates relevance and interest. You will enjoy the response you get from your students.

Now get out there and start framing your introductions to content and create a useful vision for your students. Framing will set you up for success.

There is another tool we use to promote curiosity. This second linguistic strategy is the tool that leaves your students wanting: it is an open loop.

# OPEN LOOPS

**"An open loop is a statement or action which leaves something to be completed later." - Rich Allen, PhD**

I like to use a visual metaphor to explain open loops. When you see this image in Figure 8, you notice it is a circle with openings. The mind prefers to see the complete circle and imagines the lines that fill the gaps. It turns out the mind likes and seeks closure completeness.

Metaphorically, we use an open-loop positioning statement to create a gap that makes students curious and thus wanting to close the open loop. We use open loops to set the stage for what is about to happen. We incite anticipation and create interested learners. There is a system in the brain known the reticular activating system (RAS.)[40] The RAS helps learners decide what to attend to and what to ignore. There are three categories that focus the attention of the RAS and therefore the student: physical need, self-made choice, and novelty. Novelty and choice especially make sense in that students need to respond to changes in their environment. Inserting an open loop helps to prime the students' anticipation and interest.

While I was working for an organization that was teaching a K-12 social-emotional skills curriculum, the lead trainer set out a box with a bright bow on top. She then walked up to one of the participants. She offered them a choice of a penny or a nickel. She did this again with two other participants. Then she went to a

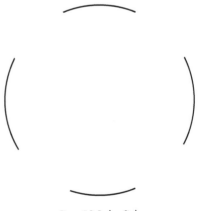

Figure # 8. Broken Circle

fourth person and made the same offer with one caveat. The participant could have all the change in the trainer's hand, or they could have the box with the bright bow sitting on the end of the desk if they waited until the end of class. At the end of the class, what was everyone so curious about? Yep, it was the box with bright bow. We all wanted to know what was in it. The trainer gave the box to the participant and they opened it to find a five-dollar bill inside. We were told that one of the greatest predictors of success later in life is delayed gratification. Then this quote (adapted from Zig Ziglar) was displayed:

**"The chief cause of unhappiness and failure is sacrificing what is wanted most, for what is wanted at the moment."**

Here's another example. I was in Alaska observing a boarding school sled shop class. Students were learning to repair snow machine engines. As the session began, the teacher passed out a carburetor to each student. When everyone had received one, he asked the students to examine the carburetors and determine what was wrong with each one. Each had something wrong with them. He told the students: "Each carburetor has some sort of problem with it—I personally saw to that. If you can tell me what is wrong, you can have this $20.00 bill. Your five minutes begins now." The students immediately began inspecting their carburetors, discussing ideas with others around them. At the end of the five minutes, no one had been able come up with a diagnosis. The teacher said: "When you are done with this class you will be able to work on snow machines with confidence. Let's learn how to repair snow machines, earn a little extra money, and keep you up and running!"

In both of these classroom examples, the teachers were using an open loop to introduce curiosity. They set the tone and piqued the students' inquisitiveness to want to know more.

Open loops come in an infinite variety of formats. As indicated in those first examples, they can simply be a statement. Other times they may be visual, such as signs or posters displayed in the room or something written on the chalkboard. An instrument placed in plain view, even though never mentioned, may serve as an open loop as long as it is used later in the class. I even leave blank areas in my handouts to be completed by the learners. All of these examples can be viewed as open loops because they serve the purpose of teasing a learners' curiosity.

Open loops make students' minds active instead of passive. Curious learners always ask questions and search for answers in their minds. Since the mind is like a muscle that becomes stronger through continual exercise, the mental exercise caused by curiosity makes your mind stronger and stronger.

The use of the open-loops linguistic strategy makes your students minds' observant of new ideas. Try this list of open loop examples in your own class:

- "In thirty seconds, when I say go…" *This is a very short-time curiosity statement used when giving directions. You will open a loop and you will close the loop, thus teaching your students they can trust you to do what you say you will do.*
- "Next up, the special ingredient that brings this all together."
- "After the break we'll be taking a look at…"
- "You don't have to believe me now, you'll see evidence of this tomorrow."
- "This side of the room, I'll talk to you in a minute. For those of you on the other side, here's a question…"
- "You'll see examples of this…"
- "We'll get to see an example of this later today."
- "Focus on this."
- "Here's how this all works."

Frames create relevance; open loops build curiosity. Below are more subtle communication directives that will create even more effectiveness in your classroom instruction.

These following positioning statements aid in creating a positive, responsive environment. The principles included here evolved over the past fifteen years and have proven to be a powerful linguistic strategy in communicating with learners in a clear, precise manner. This is where we elaborate on the *art* of our teaching practice.

## MENTAL IMAGING—DIRECTING THE FOCUS

There are two levels of processing information: conscious and nonconscious. Powerful communication can be intentional and easy. *Mental imaging* has a powerful effect on human behavior. When a person hears spoken words, the mind immediately processes that sensory data as an image. It is one of the fundamental ways you orient to the environment. The mental structuring of images allows the brain to create relationships among the objects in the physical space that senses can detect. Based on those images, choices are made on how to interact with the world. The image created in the mind's eye is often *contrary* to the idea you are attempting to communicate. In fact, it's often the *exact opposite!* Take this simple instruction—does it produce a response that is useful or harmful?

*"Class, this is the most difficult and tedious part of the chapter, so be cautious; we don't want to miss any details."*

What image does this create? Difficult, tedious, and missing details? Notice how the mental images differ with the below statement.

*"This is easily the most challenging portion of the chapter. Be attentive and patient to allow time for understanding."*

You are creating in your student's mind's eye the impression or image you have in your mind. You deliberately choose words that conjure positive associations, propel learning and enhance your communication.

Directing the focus capitalizes on the mind's ability to sort through sensory input and focus its attention. Scientists estimate that our brain receives over 10,000 bits of information every second we're awake. Once in the brain, the sensory information is processed in either a conscious or non-conscious level.[41]

Let me take this to another level. If I was to tell you, "Don't think of a pink gorilla dragging its knuckles across the floor," can you do it? If so, you are the rare one. Most of you had to push the image out of your mind to not see the pink gorilla. This is very normal. Check out these commonly used *least helpful* words:

*Can't, Won't, Don't, Shouldn't, Not, Avoid, and Never*

It's helpful for you to become aware of when and how to use these words. The images you want to eliminate often contain what could be termed as negative actions or consequences. Creating a mental image with your words is about creating awareness to the behavior that is wanted, not the behavior that is not wanted. These behaviors are usually positive or constructive. Let's look at this example: You see kids running and you say, "Don't run." The mind actually sees running. Say what you want students to do versus what you don't want them to do. If you change "Don't run" to "Walk," you are creating the mental image of the behavior you want to see. In this next statement, notice the mental images the statement focuses on.

**"Follow the directions so you don't make a lot of mistakes or you'll fail the test!"**

What two images are being created? Making mistakes and failure! Instead, the instructor might have said…

**"Be sure to focus and concentrate on the directions so that you do well on this test!"**

The image you want students to produce is "focus and concentrate."

You have the ability to put your students into a state of worry and panic or a useful mindset by careful word choice. Here's an easy one:

**"Don't forget your assignment."**

What you unintentionally directed was to "forget." Instead, say what you mean:

**"Remember your assignment."**

Try this one:

**"You are at the most difficult part of this project."**

You've directed the students to "difficult." Instead, try:

**"This is easily the most challenging part of the project that you've mastered so far."**

You want to direct the students' focus on "easily" and "mastered."

I know, some say semantics, I say cognitive linguistics. This is truly the psychology of wordsmithing. Your purposeful choice of words leads to better buy-in and cooperation.

Early in my work experience I was a lifeguard. What do you think would happen when I told the kids, "Don't run"? Yep, they walked very quickly. I needed them to be safe and I did not want them to slip or fall. I learned early on to say what I meant. I started to say, "Slow down and walk carefully." Now the mental image I was creating in their minds' eye was to slow down and be careful.

One more example from a graduate course that I was teaching at the university: I'm not proud of this moment, but it was a powerful learning experience for me. Before getting to teach at this university, we had to take a class on how to provide a rigorous university-level course. We were informed that our grading had to be on a curve. In other words, the students were expected to have a spread of grades from A – C. In effort to create some rigor into my class, I carefully selected some difficult journal articles for the students. This course was a summer one-week intensive course for teachers.

Here's what I said, "You'll notice in your syllabus the articles are taken from various credible pedagogy journals, and they are laden with research. They are hard to get through, and difficult to read." What was I thinking!?! I knew as soon as I said it, based on all the non-verbal behaviors I was seeing in my students, that I had just planted an unproductive mental image that screamed "hard to get through" and "difficult to read" mindsets. This particular group of students struggled with the readings and many didn't even try to read the articles. I worked long and hard to help them understand the articles. Thankfully, I was teaching this same course again to new students the follow week. I learned from this incident, and this was my remedy. When I handed out the syllabus, held up the optional Educational Psychology textbook and said, "The textbook for this course is about $119 and it is down at the bookstore. You can get that book if you want, however we are only here for one week and I was only going to get through part of the book. So, I copied these brief journal articles for you which speak directly to the course, and they are free." Now how would you feel? I won some goodwill capital by looking out for their best interests. The biggest difference with this class was that they actually read the articles and, more importantly, we were able to discuss them versus me telling the students what they all meant. Huge "Aha" for me. Huge. Big!

Direct the focus in your students' minds by using positive mental images of saying what you *want* or *mean* your students to do versus having them imagine what you *don't want* them to do. The reality is this: you can place your students in a mindset of failure and dread, or you can direct your students' minds to a more productive attitude.

This linguistic strategy takes practice. It is easy and quick to say, "Don't run." We often take for granted that students will assume what you mean and simply self-correct. You miss the potential to create a positive mental image for your students that is more productive than self-correction. With mental imaging, you are helping them visualize exactly what you want them to do.

## INCLUSIVENESS

Now let's talk about inclusive language positioning statements. Use inclusive language to get the reaction you want. Ever notice statements like these spoken in the classroom? "What I want you to do is take out your books." "I need you to gather your materials." "What you're going to do next is take out your homework from last night." These statements all start with "I want you to," "you're going to," and "I need you to." These lead-in statements perpetuate a me-versus-you dynamic. The message behind these statements is "I'm in control and you'll do what I say." They may have an instant negative reaction, *consciously or unconsciously*. Certain words may *unintentionally* direct a student's mind back to negative memories. You'll notice that when you use inclusive language, there is no one specifically isolated for the learner to "rebel" against. Bottom line, you are in control and you will get more cooperation by adopting inclusive words. Look at two expressions that have been rephrased to be inclusive.

I need you to take out your books. → **Let's** take out our books.

I'm going to be teaching you the steps. → **We'll** be learning these steps.

Being conscious and deliberate about the words you choose strengthens a sense of togetherness. To create a community of learners in which we all work together, it is important that your language conveys belonging and builds a sense of cooperation. Change language from "I" or "you" to "**we**" or "**us**." Instead of stating an objective using the words, "The students will," change it to, "**We will**." Rather than say, "I would like you to," say, "**Today we will**." As opposed to, "How many of you?" survey students by asking, "**How many of us?**" When your intention is to create a collaborative learning environment, use language that invites inclusion. Everything speaks, always!

Once you know you can direct a student's unconscious attention, the next question is *where* do you focus the listener's mind? Let me show you another aspect of how you can focus your student on something positive, humorous, or something that provides a new way of looking at an issue. Setting up for a photo: you want to have the tall people in the back and shorter people in the front. You could say, "All short people stand in the front." Many people have an orientation in their mind and personal experience that says "short" is potentially derogatory. Instead, you might choose this wording: "All the 'less tall' people in the front!" Delivered with appropriate humor in the voice, there's an excellent chance that good-natured laughter will follow *while the instructions are being carried out!*

We've just talked about two linguistic strategies: directing the focus with positive mental imaging language and use of inclusive language positioning statements. Our final linguistic strategy to consider is getting specific and using precise language.

## GETTING SPECIFIC

Often miscommunication results from speaking in generalities. A generality allows the other person to fill in the blanks with his or her own interpretation. The more specific your request, the greater the chance it will be accomplished according to your intention. A lack of results often stems from a lack of specifics, including your expectations about quality of work, level of interpersonal interaction, and use of resources. When information is communicated, it is interesting to note how much of it is often assumed to be understood. Frequently, miscommunication is the result of making the assumption that the listener "naturally" understands.

When I was working with Learning Forum's "SuperCamp," a ten-day learning camp, we informed our high school students that lights-out was at 11 p.m. Then we noticed chaos as everyone created their own definition of what 11 p.m. meant. We had students hanging out in the hallways or in each other's rooms in the dark. What we meant was, "Be in bed, your own bed, alone, eyes closed, at 11 p.m. sharp. Lights out is at 11 p.m." When we made our directions specific, we increased our intended results with kids in their own rooms, quiet and sleeping. In my defense, we are talking about adolescents. They sometimes have different ideas of compliance.

There is another area where specific language can make an enormous difference. When we give feedback to each other, there is a tendency to generalize the information. Specifics make feedback much more useful to the person receiving it. In addition, if we practice giving feedback with the Good, Better, Best rule,[42] the feedback now is productive and useful. Offer feedback with specifics in the form of what was "good" about what you observed, and then share what might have made it "better," followed up lastly with the "best" thing you liked. This sandwich-style tool works for all levels.

Let's look at this example: If you were acknowledging a student for a classroom presentation, you could simply say: "Well done. I liked it!" However, that kind of remark allows for no response and lacks specificity. Instead, you could say: "Excellent presentation. I enjoyed your use of metaphors and the students' reactions supported your connection to the group," thus illustrating what was "good" with specific details.

Now let's talk about criticism. If you focus on what could have made it better, the feedback is helpful without being hurtful. Here is general criticism being offered to a person.

Suppose you saw a presentation that was not well done. To be nice, you say, "That was okay." Because of the mind's tendency to generalize, the person receiving this feedback could personalize it to mean that they, *as a person,* were not very good. Instead, using a feedback "better" tool, you could say, "I felt the visual aids were difficult to see, maybe too small, and the presentation could have covered more detail." The specific feedback is helpful versus vague and uninformative.

Specific feedback offers details that allow the listener to see opportunities for improvement without feeling that their entire project was a disaster. Now follow it up with the "best" details from their presentation: "Your topic was very interesting. Your pauses and use of stories made me want to know more about what you had to say." This is a very effective strategy of giving feedback to students, teaching peers, or anyone wanting to improve.

I recently began using this sandwich style feedback with my university faculty peers. I give specific feedback using the Good, Better, Best model. I offer positive "good" feedback, identify what could be better in the middle of the sandwich, and end with what they did best. I have created four leadership development curriculums for freshman through senior undergraduate students. I share this engagement model of instructional delivery to my peers, and then I observe their classes. I see better results from the Good, Better, Best feedback sandwich model than simply identifying what was good or what could be improved.

Even at the tertiary level, I have noticed that faculty members focus on improvement and sometimes don't hear the positives. The faculty need feedback on what they do well so they can repeat those strategies. I am interested in seeing my peers keep doing what they do well, such as giving directions, using music, pacing instruction with state changes, and many other specifics that come from the engagement model. I am also interested in adding a few specific details that will give them the most bang for their time and grows their engagement success with their students. I experience more receptivity to my feedback along with the most positive acceptance to change when I use the model.

**ACCEPT PRAISE**
**AND BELIEVE IT AS**
**READILY AS YOU WOULD CRITICISM.**

## Closing Thoughts

The idea of using positioning statements is that they ultimately position the learner/listener in a more receptive, open mindset. You can empower them quickly and easily, or disengage them into disruptive tyrants. Take the road less travelled; impact your students' creativity, growth, and self-confidence to produce a group of hungry and eager learners. Mastering linguistic strategies of frames, open loops, curiosity, positive mental images, inclusive language, and specific language is a significant game changer. This part of the Engagement Model is more powerful than you might guess.

# Specific Techniques: Readiness and Responsive Approaches

Onto the final installment of the Engagement Model. As you will discover, specific techniques are the binding strategies that connect the whole engagement model. These are the fluid details we use to increase student responsiveness, promote autonomy, simplify tasks, and improve group dynamics. These strategies really drive the success of the model. As you adopt these methods, you will see where they all fit.

## STUDENT RESPONSES ➡️ DRIVE INTERACTIVE CLASSROOMS

You can make better use of your time limitations by priming students quickly for state changes, assignments, and group challenges. You'll learn the value of specifying the response for immediate informal assessment of a student's comprehension levels. The press-and-release technique will undoubtedly become a quick go-to as it allows your students a natural expression of relief and celebration after completing assigned tasks. You will appreciate their willingness to comment and respond after the release. See more information under Press and Release (#22).

Ultimately this part of the engagement model can be described as the behind-the-scenes drivers of success. While these simple practices may seem like common sense, they are not so common. Many of these techniques accelerate your students' responsiveness and expand

CHAPTER 5

the active learning process. Some are straightforward; others you will ultimately adjust and mold to fit your personality and expectations. If you want to create an inviting, engaging, collaborative experience in all your classes, these techniques will quickly and easily power up your teaching practices. You will be pleased with your students' reactions, and your gain is huge satisfaction. It's fun to use techniques with students that show immediate results.

This chapter is organized as a list of thirty-one specific techniques in alphabetical order for easy reference. These techniques are appropriate for all age levels, although you may need to be savvy about adding sophistication to older age ranges. As you read each technique, make a series of sticky notes and jot down the name as a reminder to incorporate in your teaching practices. This is quick resource guide to add to your bag of teaching tips and tricks. Enjoy!

## SPECIFIC STRATEGIES

### 1. Awareness of Comfort in Physical Situations

If you leave students in a standing pair share (which, by the way, is a great way to vary your pair shares) to give additional information, have you noticed that they begin to shift their weight or lean against something while they wait for you to finish talking? It is not comfortable to stand for very long just listening, and this is not an ideal "state" for retention. Once students are done with your standing pair share instruction, instruct them sit back down—then add information or further instruction as needed. Have you noticed when you've asked your learners to raise their hands for a response, some students keep their hands in the air or even use their other hand to hold their arm in the air? You may also need to tell them they can put their hands down.

When you lead an engager or activity that requires any kind of physical contact or touch, you want to stay aware of potential awkward feelings students may experience. However, you don't want to eliminate all uncomfortable situations due to the growth opportunities they offer your students. For example, if your activity requires students to hold hands, this creates tons of awkward feelings. Do a quick demonstration with the group holding hands and then have the students *let go* of each other's hands briefly before engaging in the challenge. Once they complete the challenge, instruct them to let go of each other's hands for the debrief or summary. Pay attention to your students when you place them in physical situations: notice fidgeting or leaning during instructions or the group debrief. When you notice, stop talking and instruct your students to get comfortable. Have them sit on chairs, desks, the floor, or return to their own desks, then finish talking or debriefing with them.

## 2. Beginnings and Endings

According to brain science theory, the brain likes beginnings and endings. Sometimes you need to wrap up one lesson and move on to other curricular demands. Do something that signifies that you're done with that topic for now. Students can operate more effectively when they are instructed that they are finished. This promotes students' full attention and presence on the next section of instruction. On a deeper and more implicit level is the need for a transition that provides a sense of completion. For instance, when students finish a paired share, have them say "Thank you" to one another. This signals that they are done talking and they are now paying attention to you for new information or instruction. You'll want to vary your endings. More ending comments your students can use include:

- Thank you.
- You rock!

- Keep up the good work!
- I get it!
- Crushin' it!

### 3. Bridges and Zones

In instructional theory, locations in the front of the class are identified as lanes of instruction. Allen[43] describes the first lane of instructional delivery as near the front board, where visual support is posted or projected. This lane of instruction is called the "Instructional Zone." The next zone, just a few feet away from the instructional zone, is called the "Dialogue Zone." This area is for less-formal instruction, discus-

sions, or even telling stories and metaphors to promote critical think-ing. The third zone is identified for mobilizing directions such as setting up a cooperative learning review activity, an engager, physical action, or simply cleaning up the room. These are the three instructional zones, or lanes, of teaching.

The "bridge" is a process that, on the surface, is similar to a behav-ioral conditioning technique. The association is considered reflexive and not a matter of choice. A bridge is the representation or signal to students that something is going to happen. For instance, occasionally student disruptions happen in the class that need group redirection. With a pre-established group discipline area or zone (this is where you might post your class rules), we physically move with "an intentional walk" to that discipline zone, thereby creating a "bridge" of association and signal to the students that bad news is coming or the class is in trouble. "Bridges and zones" is a visual connection between a zone and a behavioral pattern, learned through the experience in that zone.

### 4. Celebrations (Need I say more)

A celebration connects learners to each other with a positive expression and often with a burst of energy and enthusiasm. Play festive music that lends to the celebratory mood. Celebration is the good feeling students have about their own progress and their contributions to the learning of others. It includes the joy and excitement that infuses the classroom atmosphere. It also includes the positive acknowledgment students receive for their effort and participation. Your celebrations may be enhanced by things as small as a teacher comment expressing appreciation for accomplishment or as large as an entire group joining together in a cheer. With a sixty-second celebration, you can strengthen the learning community of the class, create connections among students, and reconnect learners to each other, the topic, and you. Have the students gather at least two favorable comments about a specific element of what you just taught or what they did. You will want to build in little celebrations too.

IF IT'S WORTH **LEARNING, IT'S WORTH CELEBRATING.**

How this might look in your class:

- Give a high-five or fist pump to others around them, followed by a round of applause.
- Pass out individual noisemakers and have students sound out celebrations.
- Use sticky-note compliments.
- Instead of clapping, have students use finger snaps when another student does or says something worthy of acknowledgment.
- Hand out giveaways (unique pencils, pens, or erasers, for ex-

ample) to the whole class. Then have students trade their item with three to five other class members with a compliment.

Ideally, celebrations will become a tradition so students will celebrate without teacher prompts. These should be an ongoing and consistent principle operating in the classroom. Celebration reinforces motivation and the message, "This is important."

### 5. Choice and Voice

Choice matters, and more so to older students; we all like having a choice. Many savvy educators allow students to control aspects of their learning, but they also work to increase students' perception of that control. You quietly choose which decisions are appropriate for the students' control, yet they feel autonomy and that their opinions are valued. A stealthy way to build in choice is to point out choices: "Today we have a choice over what to do next. Do you want to do choice A or choice B?"

Choice must be perceived as a choice in order to be a choice. Your students appreciate feeling valued for what they can contribute. This can be obvious when you ask students to help arrange a room or less obvious when you give them the opportunity to generate questions for the teacher. You can also generate ownership simply by offering students the choice to decide the order of the instruction. An example of this might be to do an activity at the beginning of the lesson or at the end of the lesson. Your students feel an increased sense of ownership when they are invited to be a part of the decision.

### 6. Contagious Role-Modeling

When we model the love of learning, show enthusiasm for our job, build suspense, smile, and tell a true personal emotional story, it lets students know what excites us. We serve as an example of values, attitudes, and behaviors associated with learning. This is especially true at the high school and tertiary levels. Contagious enthusiasm works!

**CHILDREN NEED MODELS...**

**....NOT CRITICS.**

### 7. Counterintuitive Step Back

The nature of the word "counterintuitive" implies the opposite reaction to what would seem customary. When a learner speaks in classroom settings, such as asking a question or giving an answer, it usually is important that everyone can hear clearly. Moving closer would be the spontaneous and intuitive move to make. However, this will cause the student to lower the volume of his or her voice, because you are now closer to them. Moving in the opposite direction[44] will help the student raise the volume of their voice. You will need to decide whether the rest of the class can hear the student speaking and respond by stepping back a step or two.

### 8. Deliberate Vocal Pause

Sometimes when you share a story with your classes, use a deliberate pause so that students involuntarily finish your sentence. This invites informal dialogue and promotes risk-taking. The more you offer impromptu, fill-in-the-blank opportunities for students to call out information, the more chances you have to grow a community of ownership with your deliberate pause.

### 9. Enrolling Questions

Enrolling questions are a simple technique usually started with the phrase "Raise your hand if ..." (RYHI) or "How many of you..." (HMOY). These types of questions can be applied in a variety of ways. The queries are designed to involve learners at a minimal risk level. The intention is to *enroll* our learners by bringing their background, experience, or knowledge forward and visible to the rest of the learners. We use it to gain information about students by having them raise their hands to identify if a particular statement applies to them.

If we use an enrolling question where only a few of the students have raised their hands, we can add an enrolling question similar to the initial question so that all students feel included in the conversation. For instance, if I ask students if they have ever been to Hawaii so that I can introduce riptides related to the beaches, I might say "RYHI you have ever been to Hawaii." If only a few have been to Hawaii, I simply ask, "HMOY would like to go to Hawaii?" Now everyone feels like they are part of the conversation. It is a nuance, but significant to the inclusion mindset of our learners.

**RYHI** - Raise Your Hand If....

**HMOY**- How Many Of You...

### 10. Experience Before Label

Experience Before Label influences our lesson design and delivery. It means that you involve students in an experience or elicit an experience that they can relate to before you attach a description or label. The impetus is to use teaching practices that involve the senses, perception, and memory. Experience Before

Label is about creating a teachable moment. It is about getting students emotionally involved and questioning why, when, where, what, and how.

The label in this technique refers to the information you want students to learn— facts, formulas, new terms, sequences, reasons. You demonstrate, promote discovery, and make content interactive. Telling is passive; it's not doing. Get to the doing by choosing the most important points within a given content or lecture, and devise a strategy using activities for involving students in the "discovery" of the information. These student-driven, modern classroom practices are completely different from days past. This creates a more active mental process that generates long-term retention of the information. Think experience before label. This allows learners to activate thinking processes and attach new learning to their prior knowledge. Get your students involved in a learning activity, then label the learning after they have a common experience.

## 11. Fresh, Unique, and Novel

We discussed novelty in the state change section of the book. Your students need a mixture of novel and traditional classroom routines. Habitual teaching practices help to create the predictable and safe learning environment necessary for learning and memory. The downside of predictability is that you risk boredom. The use of novelty—anything unusual or different, a fun demonstration or even a magic trick—creates a positive emotional response. To keep our teaching practices fresh, we can use unique and different strategies to balance the rou-

NOVELTY INTRIGUES, THE MIND

AND INSPIRES CURIOSITY

tine and keep learning stimulating. New challenges ignite the risk-reward dopamine system in our brains. Novel engagers are interesting because the reward chemical of dopamine release adds to our students' joy and element of surprise. Something that is novel is interesting, and something interesting is learned more easily because it is attended to.

### 12. "Front Porch" Intervention or Private Conversation

The "front porch" is a metaphor based on family conversations or important conversations that are held on the front porch of some homes. By design, it is a private talk for a conflict, a private instruction, or a private acknowledgment. You might find providing a cool, refreshing drink like lemonade or fruit punch helpful in defusing possible anxiety. Sometimes private acknowledgment for a job well done adds a nice touch of personal attention. Sometimes we need to intervene with an individual to address a conflict or behavior issue. Remember the social grace of the refreshing drink. By creating a receptive environment, we are working to disarm, deflect, deescalate and quickly redirect conflict. Asking for a front porch with a student can easily empower a learner to explain and express their needs. The cool, refreshing drink also adds a Mary Poppins effect—a spoonful of sugar helps the medicine go down—especially when you need to discuss a behavior change.

### 13. Getting Students to Respond

When you want students to go from listening mode to responding mode, you need to give them mental prep time to reply. Otherwise, you get silence as soon as you ask students if they have any questions. Waiting feels like an eternity and you decide, well, there must not be any questions or comments, so you move on with your instruction.

Oftentimes we need to give students time to prepare. This is easily accomplished by using a quick pair or trio share to have a brief discussion with other students about how you want them to verbally respond. Taking students from listening mode to talking mode[45] makes the transition to classroom discussion richer and more meaningful. A side benefit is that this practice often shapes a key social-emotional skill of building confidence in your students.

## 14. Gradual Volume Voice Reduction

You can redirect a talking classroom by intentionally reducing the volume of their voices. You develop your own assertive statement that can be used as a signal for redirection. Begin your assertive statement by projecting your voice (this is not shouting) with a strong, bold volume, gradually decreasing to a volume level equal to your normal instructional or conversational voice.

I use these assertive statements: "pause your conversations," "hold that thought," "where you are at right now is perfectly fine." Then I begin the gradual reduction in my tone and voice to where I have all the students' attention. Bringing students from conversation to instruction is a simple refocusing technique. Once you have your students' attention, instruct them with a completion statement like "Please say 'thank you' to your partners." Usually all the students are finished with their conversations and I am ready to move them to my next directive or content section. All this is done with a positive inflection, keeping the instructional zone positive.

### 15. If Telling Were the Same as Teaching, We Would All Be So Smart (Pat Wolfe)

Telling students all the answers in a passive, sit-and-get learning format isn't really teaching, it's telling. You first choose the most important points within a given content or lecture, and then devise a strategy for *involving* the students in the discovering of the information, instead of simply telling them. This creates an active mental process that is more likely to generate long-term retention of the information.

### 16. Impeccability

Impeccability is the way you show up in your teaching—your energy, appearance, bulletin boards, walls, room setup, and preparation. The neatness and cleanliness of these factors sends a message about your commitment and expectations of yourself and your students alike. There is a subconscious expectation that what I am teaching and sharing has value. Your ability to teach with impeccability sets a tone of quality and purpose. By being constantly aware of this important principle, you tend to be more deliberate and proactive in coordinating the messages students receive. Everything from your environment to your body language sends a message. Everything speaks. Everything!

### 17. Layering

Scaffolding education is not a new concept. When you want your students to learn, you scaffold, or layer, information to add to their prior knowledge.

Layering refers to the structure you use to communicate a specific sequence of steps in a lesson or an activity. The purpose is to assist in the development of a central idea through a sequential, deliberate addition of new elements to what is already known.[46] It turns out that when we give students too many directives, they inevitably leave a few directions out (as we discussed in Chapter 1). Layering means taking a given set of directions and using a progression model that layers in the given rules (directives) in a timely fashion so all the steps are followed.

For instance, in an engager named Hand Hacky (see Appendix B, #18), the group is to tap a hacky sack (with hands instead of feet) into the air, trying to keep it from hitting the floor. The next step added is to cheer and applaud when the hacky hits the floor. After the group practices this step, a final step is added to have the group count how many times they can keep the hacky in the air while still cheering and applauding when it hits the ground. When I have led this activity and given all the directions at the same time, the groups notoriously leave out one step—the cheering and applauding when the hacky hits the ground.

This is important for a content game I teach immediately following the hand-hacky engager. I need the group to cheer and applaud when they have completed a round of the challenge. By having the students' practice it layered into the hand-hacky game, I essentially increase the likelihood that students will carry that expectation to the next activity. Layering the directions with a practice step for all sections of a multi-step challenge adds to a successful experience. Everything you do is for a purpose.

## 18. Labeling Words to be Avoided

Certain labeling words in learning situations can be counterproductive. There are multiple definitions of common words such as work, energy, size, shape, and growth. When a label is spoken by a teacher, learners immediately bring to mind their past experiences related to that label. For better or worse, they mentally prepare themselves for what they *believe* to be the worst.

This in itself doesn't set you up for a poor experience with a potential activity or lesson. With younger students, the words *sing, dance,* or *play* usually are not perceived as negative. Younger students do get very excited about those labels, which may or may not be what you intend. However, when you move up to middle, high school, and post-secondary levels, students may associate *sing, dance,* or *play* labels with threatening, anxiety-producing, or unpleasant previous experiences. You'll find that some middle school and most high school students are peer-driven; if they think anything will potentially embarrass them, they simply will not participate. Even using the label *play* with a group of administrators is going to get you some eye-rolling and low groans of disapproval. You'll find yourselves explaining all the details just to gain buy-in and usually giving away the value and discovery potential.

Instead, instruct the students to stand up, and simply share that physical movement holds value in your ability to recall content. As they are standing, model a few physical movements and have students copy you. Then add music. *Voila!* you are now dancing, albeit not hip dancing, but it does look like dancing. Your students are laughing, moving, getting a kinesthetic hit, and changing the energy of the room in a productive manner for learning! The label word "dancing" was never mentioned.

### 19. Note Taking

When learners take written notes, much more is happening than most teachers realize. The process of taking in, analyzing, and recording new information is a challenging enterprise for many learners, and its complexity is far too often overlooked. You can build confidence and recall by building in time to honor the note-taking process. As you see your students taking notes, pause your instruction so not to interfere with their concentration. As much as you think you can multitask, your students can get lost trying to take effective notes and understand at the same time.

To honor successful note-taking:

- Build in effective pauses
- Build in effective review opportunities
- Build in effective state changes
- Build in effective novelty (highlighting/writing in colors or use of stars, exclamation marks and symbols)

### 20. Pause for Visuals[47]

When your information is visually presented to your students with a PowerPoint slide, document camera or other format, they must be given time to familiarize the information in their mind. If you allow time (a brief moment) for learners to mentally organize an image of what you have shared to get the BIG PICTURE before you begin explaining the material, students will retain more of the content or concept. Pausing briefly, then adding instruction or clarification gives your students time to process visual information and enables better comprehension of the content. When we ask our students to listen to us talk while they are looking at the image or words, we distract them from both. It turns out that we can't pay attention to two things at the same time; what ends up happening is interference with students' retention potential.

PAUSE FOR VISUALS

CHAPTER 5

### 21. Practice Grace

When you practice grace, you have a responsive mindset that allows for patience, forgiveness, and acceptance of where students are in the developmental process. Challenging behavior occurs when the demands of the environment exceed a student's capacity to respond adaptively. Many popular explanations for challenging behavior place blame on the learner or his or her parents. Typically, students' behavior occurs for a purpose. They are looking for ways to belong, feel significant, and self-protect.

When learners perceive a threat to their self-esteem, a downward spiral can begin. Students can be led into obstructive behaviors in the faulty belief that this will gain them a place of belonging and significance. How we respond to inappropriate behaviors can determine how entrenched

they become. The secret is to break them out of the spiral by supporting their real needs without supporting their destructive, faulty beliefs and alienating patterns of reaction. The idea of cooperative behavior is your ability to be responsive, not punitive. Commit yourself to a win-win approach even if tactics used by the student are manipulative. Be clear that your task is to steer the negotiation in a positive direction.

### 22. Press and Release[48]

Press and Release serves as a metaphor in which you press the students in content delivery or use of an engager—times when you expect learners to fully concentrate. It can feel like pressure. Extended periods of *pressing* can cause learners to become fidgety and restless. This results in a need for some kind of *release*.

The more creative the *release,* the better. For instance, use an activity or event to bring students back to a more manageable state to focus. A simple press-and-release scenario has to do with sitting and listening too long. To release that pressure, ask students to stand up for a paired share involving questions reflected by the content covered. Another place where a press-and-release moment can be appropriate is during an intense problem-solving activity or project where all students had to remain silent for an extended amount of time. Again, a simple *release* could be to give each other a physical acknowledgment such as a high five, coupled with a statement such as "we're good!" After the release action, most of your students will want to talk about their experience with each other and the group as a whole. The trick comes with reading the pressure you have created and in a timely manner offer the release. You'll love it!

### 23. Prevent One-Word or No Answers

The goal of preventing one-word answers is to open a discussion with your students. One-word answers suggest there is only one right answer. Sometimes in your instruction that is the case, but when you want to engage the whole class in the discussion, you may want to allow for multiple right answers.

When you ask a question in a *closed* format it indicates there is a single correct response. For example, "Which leadership theory is authoritarian?" Simply by changing a question to an *open* format, you allow students to have several options in their response. For example, "Which leadership theory resonates with you and why?" indicates there is more than one possible answer. Here's another: "What do you know about the character in this story based on his actions and what he said?" Use an open questioning format to allow for deeper levels of processing and discussion, which in turn will instigate higher levels of discussion and engagement.

It's a simple tweak. Begin with the following words or phrases: why, how, what, describe, "tell me about," or "what do you think about…" Although "tell me about" does not begin as a question, the result is the same as asking an open-ended question. How about that!

### 24. Priming

Priming allows students to be prepared for the next instruction from the teacher.[49] It helps avoid those brief but awkward moments during instruction when learners fully intend to respond, yet find themselves unable to complete the request because they need to complete something else first, like writing a note. It is necessary to prime or ready students by asking them to put down their pencils or pens before proceeding with the next instruction.

For instance, as a graduate student I attended a panel discussion about becoming a professor for a research university, a liberal college, or community college. We were an attentive audience, madly taking notes. When the panel was done speaking, the lead professor asked us to give our guests applause. Some of us were still writing; some were clapping with pens in their hands. He had to ask us again to give the panel a "hearty" applause. We were not trying to be unappreciative, just trying to finish writing a few notes. If the professor had primed us by saying, "I know you are busily finishing your notes. Can we quickly put our pens down, give our panel a hearty applause and then you can return to finishing your notes." Sometimes a simple priming command will quickly accomplish a needed task without having to go into redirections or disappointment in your students.

### 25. Specify the Response[50]

Have you ever seen the following in a classroom: the teacher stops in the middle of teaching and asks students, "Did you get that?"

How are your students supposed to respond to you? Raise their hands, nod their heads in agreement, or stand up and say, "I got it?" In the game of school, it is assumed that students know how to respond. However, in these situations, teachers must specify *how* learners are expected to respond. For example: raise your hand if you need more time.

This technique generates a heightened sense of reassurance in the classroom and may even lead to increased levels of participation by less-confident learners. That's the bigger picture for this strategy. On a simpler scale, let me describe this technique another way. If you want to find out if everyone one in the class has a pencil or pen and is ready to begin, you can ask, "Does everyone have a pen?" Or you can *specify the response* by asking your students, "If you have a pen or pencil, hold it in the air." This way, you can see who is ready and who still needs time without embarrassing them. The same strategy works when you want to find out who in the class doesn't have something they need. By having students hold a book or an object in the air to signal that they do indeed have it, you can see who needs help. Now you can arrange to get the book or object to that student without drawing unwanted or negative attention to them. Remember, "specify the response" is how you want your students to respond to your questions.

## 26. The Sandwich Question Format

When you ask your students a question that you want to use to instigate a discussion, you already know it takes a few moments for them to formulate responses before offering their answers. This sandwich format offers another seamless effect in getting a quick response. Ready your students by first asking the question to set up the overall question; second, offer information and details to clarify types of responses you expect; and third, ask the very same question to jumpstart the discussion. You will eliminate the immediate pause you receive when you ask questions. Here's an example:

> *What are some of the ways you might you use state changes in your teaching environments?*
> *Maybe a pair share, stand up and stretch…*
> *What are some of the ways you might you use state changes in your teaching environments?*

### Ask a Question / Clarify with Detail / Ask the Original Question

**First:**

Ask the group a question

**Second:**

Give the group some clarifying information
without giving the answer away

**Third:**

Then ask the very same question

## 27. Turn To

You can create great positive psychological value in the classroom by creating student-to-student acknowledgment and quick social grouping as a critical part of a positive and energized learning environment. Following any pair-share, interview, review of prior learning, or group work, incorporate a social cue/greeting with the use of "turn-tos." Here's an example: once the engaged activity or conversation is complete, have students "turn to" the student(s) they are working with and say, "Good job," "You did great," "Thank you," and so on. Include a physical salutation like a high five, fist pump, or elbow bump. "Turn to" is another variation of completions combined with acknowledgments. Turn to someone near you now and say, "I get it!"

## 28. Use Rituals and Routines

The use of rituals serves many purposes, from time-savers to predictability and increased psychological security for learners. Rituals in your classroom can instantly engage learners.

Oftentimes we never know what happened in the hallway on the way to our class. At the start of class, students could still be distracted from that interaction. It could be an insult, a breakup with a close friend, a fight, or the loss of something valuable. Using dependable activities that trigger specific, predictable states can be the perfect way to connect to the class and get mentally present for the instruction. The mind likes patterns and looks for them to conserve cognitive decision-making energy. Routines provide that very nicely for us and our learners.

Make these habits quick and change them weekly to keep it fun. When I was teaching at the university, I opened all my classes with a ritual engager. Sometimes it was up and moving, sometimes it was a mind teaser, and sometimes it was a personal reflection. I was worried that many students would come late to class, but I found just the opposite. My students commented that they always wanted to be on time because they were afraid they would miss something. The daily routines you use will create dependable anticipation that keeps stress levels low and reduces threat responses. Each morning, you can have a "getting ready to learn" time or a special song used with positive greetings, special handshakes, hugs, or sharing time. During the day, use high levels of novelty and movement. Consider organizational rituals such as cheers, gestures, and mini-games, or applause affirmations such as one clap, two claps, finger snaps, or a silent cheer. Lastly, consider using closure or summary rituals to help students finish the week (see closure activities in the Appendix). After all, we tend to be creatures of habit!

## 29. Vary the Visual Field

The visual field is the place in the classroom where a teacher leads the instruction. One of the advantages of changing students' visual field is that it acts as an attention-getter. When you shift to a new position in the room and teach from that space, you vary your students' visual field. This change cues your students to be mentally alert. Occasional changes in the visual field of the classroom can help students remain focused on the content as well. This gives teaching from all sides of the room a new meaning. Vary that visual field!

# Is Your Teaching Memorable?

## "Memory is the ART of Attention"
## "All Learning is Remembering"

How many of you have a really good memory? How many of you have a medium memory: some things you remember, some things you forget? How many of you can't remember what kind of memory you have? Sometimes I think that as educators, we fall into the trap of "hope." *After all, I told them it would be on the test. I showed them a PowerPoint. I made a visual.* We hope students will remember.

The truth is that memory is the art of attention, and all learning is remembering. Our memory is based on recall mechanisms that remind us of something else. We also create mental triggers in the environment to help us remember. Your job is to use what we know about how memory works, organizes, and stores itself in the brain with your instruction.

Educational researchers agree that emotions have a significant effect on our recall. As teachers, we can vastly improve student recall by connecting content with positive emotions and teaching our students to use and develop reminder triggers.

How short is short-term memory?

- ☐ Five to fifteen seconds
- ☐ One to two minutes
- ☐ One two hours

That's right: five to fifteen seconds is how long our short-term memory holds on to information. Short-term memory is like a buffer zone; it fills up rapidly and empties just as quickly. How much information can we hold in short-term memory? As it turns out, NOT MUCH. Research suggests only five to nine items (or chunks) of informaton can be accomomondated at a time.[51]

The size of the chunk depends on the prior knowledge of the learner. For instance, is the number 907 one item or three items? Answer: it depends. If you process the number as an area code in Alaska, you process it as a single chunk. Chunking decreases the number of items you are holding in memory by increasing the size of each item. Instead of trying to remember the string of ten numbers individually, it is easier to remember by grouping or chunking them as 450.598.8356. Therefore, instead of remembering ten individual numbers, you are remembering three larger chunks. For learning purposes, it's why we work to create meaningful chunks that condense several pieces of information into one chunk.

There's no such thing as a bad memory. We have a trained memory or an untrained memory. Brain scientists call this "neuroplasticity." This simply means when we exercise our minds, we can repair, rejuvenate and ENHANCE our mental abilities to a higher level, no matter where we start.

Scientists estimate that each of us has the lifelong capacity to make up to 500 trillion new brain connections among our neurons, yet most of us take advantage of less than one percent of our true mental potential.[52]

Your memory is one of your greatest advantages and the foundation of all achievement. Our memories make up who we are; they shape our knowledge and attitudes.

The brain is like a mental muscle; it grows stronger with use. The problem is that we're outsourcing our brain to our digital devices. In extreme cases, this results in "digital dementia."[53]

'Digital dementia' is a term coined by neuroscientist Manfred Spitzer to describe an overuse of digital technology resulting in the breakdown of cognitive abilities. Spitzer proposes that short-term memory pathways will start to deteriorate from underuse if we overuse technology. Although, in this blog, we have recently explored outsourcing your memory to smartphones, these two concepts are different—the mental disarray within the brain implied by the term 'dementia' is far more basic and complete. An under-practiced memory process is far from being comparable to the wider cognitive devastation that is dementia.

Many of us store information on our digital devices. When we store all our information, it becomes our memory because we can look up any information we need at the moment. We use our phones' calculator to do math including tips and discounts, our phones' mapping GPS to get around town, and our calendars to manage our schedule. Knowledge is po-

**MEMORIES ARE MALLEABLE.**

PLAY IT AGAIN SAM !

tential power that only becomes power when we act on it. Here are a few concepts about memory that will inform your teaching.

## MEMORY AND TEACHING

While there is plenty of research and information about memory, I am focusing on how I use it in my classrooms and how you may use it in yours. For our purposes, we'll look at Primacy and Recency, Chunking, Familiarity, Visualization, and Mnemonic Techniques. Mnemonic techniques are considered elaborate rehearsal memory techniques that enhance memory and recall. Repetition is still needed, but much less than if you rely on rote memory rehearsal alone.

Memory is the art of attention. Our goal here is to help learners be present and keep them in a positive state. Powerful presence comes from being powerfully present. Let's dive in and start remembering!

**Primacy and Recency**

What is presented or taught at the beginning of a lesson has the best chance of being remembered. This is known as "recency."

In *Memory: A Contribution to Experimental Psychology (1885)*, Ebbinghaus noted that people are far more likely to remember items at the start and end of lists. He refers to these effects as *primacy* and *recency*. The principle is that material from each end of a learning experience is retained more than the information taught in the middle. This has been confirmed many times since. In a specific experiment by E.J Thomas in *Studies in Adult Education*,[54] it was found that there was a massive dip in attention and recall from the middle of lectures. In other words, in lectures and the classroom, the effects of primacy and recency are profound.

The **recency effect** is remembering best the items at the end of a list or lesson. Evidence of this shows up in textbook chapters in the form of a short summary at the beginning and end of chapters. The primacy-recency implication for content delivery is that new material should be followed by practice or review before moving on. At this point, the information is no longer new, and the practice helps the learner organize it for further processing. The summary should take place at the end of instruction since this is the second most powerful learning position (after primacy) and an important opportunity for the learner to determine sense and meaning. Adding summary activities to the end of the lesson shows how we can take advantage of research on retention to design a more effective lesson.

## Chunking (7±2)

Chunking is the technique of breaking information down into groups or units. According to Miller, the capacity of short-term memory (STM) is seven, plus or minus two.[55] This is the *number of chunks of information* a person can hold in working memory at the same time, where a chunk is any meaningful item. This is based on the idea that STM is limited in the number of things that can be retained. If you try to remember groups of items in chunks of more than nine, your brain gets confused.

## Familiarity, Emotion, and the Unusual

STM is so limited that items must clamor for attention. We use emotion, personal interest, or the unusual to extend our working memory's capabilities, either by rehearsal (mental repetition), rote memory, or chunking into smaller bits of information and associating it with something meaningful.

## "Imagination is more powerful than knowledge."
### – Albert Einstein

**Visualization**

Thinking in pictures is the universal language. Try this: close your eyes and think of an apple. Open your eyes and answer these questions. What did you see? Did you see the word "APPLE?" Did you see a picture of an apple? Was it in black and white or color? What color apple did you see?

According to a study published in the Journal of Neuroscience, when we look at a known word, our brain sees it like a picture, not a group of letters needing to be processed. The study's senior author, Maximilian Riesenhuber, PhD, says that "Neurons respond differently to real words, such as turf, than to nonsense words, such as turt, showing that a small area of the brain is 'holistically tuned' to recognize complete words."[56]

# MNEMONIC TECHNIQUES

A mnemonic technique acts as a "hook" (holding place of sorts, a recall trigger) by which the student can pull the needed information out of long-term memory and into conscious memory. Memory retrieval increases with multiple and varied modes of instruction of the same material.

**More Complex Material Needs More Complex Mnemonics**

Simpler mnemonic strategies such as rhymes, keywords, acronyms, and acrostics work well with limited amounts of material. Usually a rhyme or alliterative phrase is tied to one particular fact and keywords are most often used to remember individual difficult or foreign words. Acronyms and acrostics, due to their nature, usually encompass more material, but rarely will you find an acronym or acrostic that's longer than six or seven letters (in the case of acronyms) or words (in the case of acrostic sentences). The number of items an acronym or acrostic can bring back to mind is limited. For example, Roy G Biv is an acronym used for the sequence of hues described in a rainbow. HOMES is used as an acronym for the five Great Lakes: Huron, Ontario, Michigan, Erie, and Superior. The last one, EGBDF, is used to help remember the treble clef for music notes: Every Good Boy Does Fine. You get it.

### Three Powerful Mnemonic Strategies

There *are* ways to tie many more than six or seven items into the same mnemonic. Three of the most popular ways to do so are the loci method, storytelling method, and the pegword method. These three strategies not only allow you to tie many items together into one mnemonic, but they also allow you to remember that material in a particular order.

Fortunately, I learned the power of mnemonic strategies in graduate school. My friend Rich Allen and I were taking a learning theories class at Arizona State University. The professor said, "I have been teaching for the last twenty-four years; I talk, you listen; there will be a midterm and a final exam for your grades. I will talk for about an hour and a half, then you may ask questions." I was sunk. Rich helped me create a study guide and adapted a mnemonic technique to help me remember all the learning theories. As luck would have it, I passed the class.

Then I worked a few summers at Learning Forum (SuperCamp), where we taught the very same mnemonic techniques to high-school age campers. These techniques are so simple they tend to get overlooked for their value. Note that the information being taught to students needs to be encoded, then you use the mnemonic to aid in recall. For example, when teaching the order of operations, math teachers use the acronym PEMDAS (Please Excuse My Dear Aunt Sally) to help students remember the order in which to solve math equations. After your instruction, using a mnemonic acts as a powerful retrieval mechanism.

### *The Loci method*

The Loci (place) method is based on an ancient Greek memory technique attributed to Simonides of Ceos, who lived 2500 years ago, the only survivor of a building collapse during a dinner he attended. Simonides was able to identify the dead, who were crushed beyond recognition, by remembering where the guests had been sitting. The loci system was used as a memory tool by both Greek and Roman orators to give speeches without the aid of notes. It remained the most popular mnemonic system until about the mid-1600s, when the phonetic and peg systems were introduced.

**Locus** is Latin for "location," and "loci" is the plural form. It is based on the assumption that you can best remember places that you are familiar with. If you link something you need to remember with a place that you know very well, the location will serve as a recall tool.

The method of loci is essentially a visual filing system, helping you to memorize and recall an almost unlimited number of items in a fixed order. Each location serves as a holding place you visually connect to whatever you want to remember. You accomplish this by creating an image or scene in which the location and the to-be-memorized item are associated. For instance, I use my home.

Think of a well-known place that you can visualize in great detail. Many people use their house or a room; I have the students use their bedrooms. However, you could use a favorite place in your memory like the house you grew up in or your drive to work every day (if you drive the same way on a daily basis.)

Let's give it a try! Here is a list of ten items I want to remember; I am using my home as an example. I imagine myself parking in my (1) *driveway*, walking up to the (2) *front porch*, entering through the (3) *front (red) door*, walking into my (4) *living room*, past my (5) *wine rack,* through the (6) *office hallway*. I enter my office; first is my (7) *bookcase*, across from my (8) *plant table*, across from my (9) *desk*, and overhead is my (10) *ceiling fan*. This gives me

1. Driveway
2. Front Porch
3. Front Door (Red)
4. Living Room
5. Wine Rack
6. Office Hallway
7. Office Bookcase
8. Plant Table
9. Desk
10. Ceiling Fan

ten locations in my home that I can use as recall triggers to mentally file ten items.

I imagine walking through my home to make sure I always use the same locations in the same order. Now I can use my home as loci (places) to attach any information I want to remember. Using this loci method, I can remember ten items over an extended time.

Now that you know the basics, try to apply the method of loci in your daily life. You can start with your house, garden, or a familiar route through your city. Then use it to remember your to-do-list, a grocery list, the key points of a magazine article you are reading, or content you want to teach. Teach your students how to use this to memorize information for a test heavy on content. Science, social studies, language arts rules—let your imagination guide you.

### Storytelling links

Storytelling (also called linking or chaining) is the use of multiple keywords in a linked association. With this method, the material is told in a story format that is logically linked. The storytelling "link" will tie material together if it needs to be remembered in a particular order. Each word or idea you must remember cues the next idea you need to recall.

For example, if you had to remember the words "cup," "table," "cat," "butter," and "camera," you could create a linking story that had a cup falling off a table onto a cat that was standing in butter, and you took a picture of it with a camera. All linking does is make one item of information the trigger for the next piece of information. Focus on the key points of what you're learning and arrange them in a logical sequence. Link them with a story so that when you retell the story either out loud or silently to yourself, the story links act as the recall trigger. Here's a practical sample using typical science content—the mineral hardness scale—moving from softest to hardest.

1. Talc
2. Gypsum
3. Calcite
4. Fluorite
5. Apatite
6. Feldspar (Orthoclase)
7. Quartz
8. Topaz
9. Corundum
10. Diamonds

Jessy poured (Talc)um powder onto a (Gypsum's) head, who cried out in pain right before she turned into a (Calcite) statue. Along came an artist who decided to polish the statue's teeth with a (Fluorite) cloth. The artist grew a huge (Apatite) and immediately ordered a pizza with (Feldspar) and pineapple. Upon delivery, the artist accidently dropped the pizza on the (Quartz) floor. (Topaz) the dog ran off with the pizza, putting the artist into a (Corundum). Then the statue broke open and (Diamonds) fell and sparkled all the way to the ground. The artist suddenly forgot his hunger.

Students practice their created story by sharing it with several other students. This elaborative memory rehearsal technique of storytelling now becomes the recall mechanism to remember the mineral hardness scale in order from softest to hardest. Your students will amaze themselves and impress their peers and their parents.

### *Peg system*

A "peg" is a mental hook on which you hang information. This hook acts as a reminder to help you retrieve that information. As with the previous two mnemonic methods, peg memory systems are ideal for remembering material that must be recalled in a particular order. Pegs work by associating information you already know (the numbers 1 through 20 and the letters A through Z) with new facts you want to remember. This is an ideal device to use with older students. If you use this method with elementary students, the peg lists need to be shorter and incorporate rhymes (one is bun, two is  shoe, three is tree, for is floor, five is hive, and so on). The association words used in the following pages are associations and rhymes.

A peg system works in two stages. First, you pre-memorize a list of keywords with corresponding kinesthetic hand motions; this becomes your master pegword list. You can use the same list of keywords and hand motions to memorize a variety of content. Generally, your master peg list only has to be memorized one time, then you can use it over and over with a new list of items you want to memorize.

The list I was taught includes twenty items (there are many different twenty-item pegword lists out there and a number of ten-item lists as well. Choose the association words that make the most sense to you). A twenty-word peg-list allows you to "peg," or memorize, up to twenty items. The peg-lists are generated from words that are easy to associate with the accompanying number. For some of these items, use rhymes such as one-sun, six-sticks, nine-line and ten-hen. For others, there is a logical relationship like two eyes, three sides on a triangle or four burners on a standard cooktop.

Here is my peg-list with the corresponding hand gesture. Saying the number and the associated object out loud while adding the physical hand gesture motion at the same time will increase your memory storage of the list. This kinesthetic element is not found in other mnemonic strategies. The importance of using hand gestures as your kinesthetic element is a necessary step to aid recall of the information.

**Step one: Memorize this peg-list and use the kinesthetic tips to help you anchor the pegs.**

Practice the list below by adding the physical movement and saying the item out loud. For example, you say, "One is sun," while taking each hand, starting out together in front of your face, and moving them outward and down in an arc to each side, outlining the shape of the sun on the horizon at sunrise or sunset. Next, say, "Two is eyes," while pointing with two fingers on one hand your pointer and middle finger—the shape of a peace sign—at your eyes, then moving them rapidly away from you. And so on. It only takes a few minutes of repetition and saying it out loud (working with a friend who can quiz you helps) to learn the whole peg-list quickly.

The cerebellum is in charge of muscle or physical memory, like riding a bike. When it comes time to recall the information and you get stuck, use the hand motion that is associated with that peg to activate your recall. As soon as you do the hand motion, the image will pop back into your mind along with the material you pegged. Say the number first, use a hand gesture motion, then say the item. Your turn. Ready, go.

1. One is Sun – Draw a circle in the air with both hands (top to bottom). Say "Sun."

2. Two is Eyes – One hand with your index finger and the middle finger (peace sign) at your eyes, moving them rapidly away from you. Say "Eyes."

3. Three is Triangle – Using your index fingers at an imaginary apex, draw in the air the lines of a triangle. Say "Triangle."

4. Four is Stove – Use the palm of your hand and place your palm over each of the imaginary four burners on a standard cook top. Say "Stove."

5. Five is Fingers – Wave five fingers in the air. Say "Fingers."

6. Six is Sticks – Bend at the waist, using one hand to pick up imaginary sticks. Say "Sticks."

7. Seven is 7-UP – Using an imaginary big soda, turn up a can to take a big drink. Say "7-UP."

8. Eight is Octopus – Waving both hands to the side like an octopus in the ocean. Say "Octopus."

9. Nine is Line – Using one hand draw a straight line from the top of your reach to your waist. Say "Line."

10. Ten is Hen – Place both hands on your sides in a wing fashion moving up to down. Say "Hen."

11. Eleven is Fence – Place your index fingers together, alternating them from left to right in an imaginary picket fence. Say "Fence."

12. Twelve is Eggs – Place your hands together like you're holding an egg high and bring them down as if you broke the egg open. Say "Eggs."

13. Thirteen is Cat – Imagine petting a black cat; the association is black and unlucky. Say "Cat."

14. Fourteen is Heart – Place your index fingers in front of you, drawing an imaginary heart. Say "Heart."

15. Fifteen is Fame – One hand high, one hand low as in a fame pose (Andy Warhol said everyone would have 15 minutes of fame). Say "Fame."

16. Sixteen is Drive – Place both hands on an imaginary steering wheel and make a driving motion (in the U.S., we can get a driver's license at 16 years old). Say "Drive."

17. Seventeen is Magazine – Hold hands as if holding an imaginary magazine (*Seventeen* is a popular teen magazine). Say "Magazine."

18. Eighteen is Vote – Using one hand, move index finger in them motion of a check mark (in the U.S., we can legally vote at age eighteen). Say "Vote."

19. Nineteen is Remote – Remote rhymes with Vote. Point an imaginary remote at a TV. Say "Remote."

20. Twenty is 20/20 Vision – Use both hands as if holding a pair of binoculars up to your eyes. Say "20/20 Vision."

That's step one. For your information, notice the list is broken up in chunks of five. This is chunking ($7\pm2$) for short-term/working memory utilization. Work to learn and memorize this master list in chunks of five. **Step two: link the content you want to recall to your peg-list.**

Here's a mini-example of five items. (1) Learning is State Dependent, (2) Turn it UP! Climate Control, (3) Social-Emotional Mindfulness, (4) Linguistic Strategies (5) Specific Techniques.

1. Draw a circle in the air with both hands (top to bottom) visualizing the Sun. Say One is "Learning is 'State' Dependent."

2. With one hand, point your index finger and the middle finger into a peace sign. Point the peace sign at your eyes, then move it rapidly away. Saying Two is "Turn It UP! Climate control."

3. Using your index fingers at an imaginary apex, draw in the air the lines of a triangle visualizing a triangle. Say Three is "Social-Emotional Mindfulness."

4. Place the palm of your hand over each of the imaginary four burners on a standard cook top. Say Four is "Linguistic Strategies."

5. Wave five fingers in the air. Say Five is "Specific Techniques."

You just "pegged" the engagement model elements behind this whole book. That's the gist of associating the context or content to the peg. Once you get used to the process, it really doesn't take long to create a set of visualizations that help you recall long lists of information or concepts in a specific order. Although this was a numbered peg system; there are alphabet peg systems too. Check the internet for more great ideas.

Peg systems provide a big advantage over free recall (rote memorization). The pegs serve as a recall method for you to remember random items. Another upside of using the peg system is that it can be used over and over. An incredible truth about your brain is that it can distinguish between the same numerical list (pegs) being used multiple times for different information. Spacing out the use of the lists and combining the use of pegs with the other memory systems lets you use pegs to memorize a very large body of information. Pegs can also be combined with the loci or storytelling link systems. Combining peg systems with other memory systems allows you to memorize huge amounts of information.

## Closing Thoughts

I used a peg system to memorize all the learning theories for a master's level course my first year of school. Remember the professor who said he would talk, we would listen? I failed my midterm. Fortunately for me, he was only interested in me learning the information, and not punishing my poor study skills. I was able to take the class and the exams as many times as I wanted within a year of my first class. Lucky for me, Rich Allen was in the very same class. He taught me the peg system and helped me lay out all the learning theories in an easy to study system, such as color coding the theories with identical highlighters and grouping facts and information as it related to the theory. Then I used the peg system to memorize all the theories. If you had been there, you may have thought I had lost my mind while I was taking my test. I would make the hand gesture motions with each peg to help me recall all the facts and important details I had studied to pass the test. It worked!

As you digest this cool memory information, I hope you're thinking of ways you can incorporate mnemonics into your own teaching practices. You will grow your students' confidence. They will be impressed with how much they can recall. Ask yourself: is your teaching memorable? Try it, you might just surprise yourself!

## FOUR THINGS YOU CAN DO RIGHT NOW

1. Practice makes Progress—start today.
2. Memory is not a noun, it's something you do.
3. Powerful presence comes from being powerfully present—memory is the art of attention.
4. Teach your students about how their memory works.

# Lesson Design and Planning

In this chapter, I want to discuss the Five-Part Model[57] for lesson planning. The model serves as a blueprint to aid the use of music, frames, state changes, specific techniques, and curiosity positioning statements in your lessons. This is basically a template for interactive learning environments that boosts the delivery of any content.

## A BRIEF LESSON MODEL FOR INTERACTIVE LEARNING ENVIRONMENTS

| The Step | Time (in Minutes) | Purpose |
|---|---|---|
| (1) Engager | 2-5 | Engage the students' attention. |
| (2) Frame | Less than 1 | Create a perspective. |
| (3) Activity | 5-30 | Bring about a conceptual awareness. |
| (4) Debrief | 5-15 | Highlight major points for discussion. |
| (5) Metaphor | 2-5 | Relate key ideas to a broader perspective. |

Note this sequence is only a *model* of how an engaging lesson plan could be designed. Times for each step may vary, the sequence itself may be adjusted, or some steps may even be eliminated. Teachers should adapt the general format to meet their individual needs.

### 1. Engager—Prepare the Mind/Body for Learning

The primary purpose of an engager is to mentally prepare your students for the learning session. Engagers (or "energizers") are used

137

to bring participants into the moment, to temporarily remove distractions, and reduce any perceived anxiety of the setting. We use an engager to help our students stay present.

## 2. Frame—Establish the Relevance of the Learning Material

We position content with a "frame statement" (see Chapter 4, Linguistic Strategies) to address students' concerns so they can focus on the learning and explain the immediate learning objective(s). The frame should answer the following questions:

Why am I here?

What am I supposed to learn?

How is this information important to me?

How will this new knowledge benefit me?

## 3. Activity/Explore/Content—Involve and Engage the Student in the Material

This step introduces students into the key content of our training—NOT by telling them about it, but by involving them in it. Use activities that include sensory experiences and attention. This type of active exploration is vital when we stimulate learners on multiple levels—physically, mentally, socially, emotionally—improving their comprehension and recall.

## 4. Debrief—Process the Experience and Relate to Personal Learning

The debrief highlights and reinforces the key points of your lesson. It typically involves facilitating student dialogue or interaction relating to the prior exploration activity. This helps you determine what content students have internalized and what needs to be elaborated further. The key in this stage is to guide students toward a clear understanding of the content. See the following section on debriefing and processing for specific concepts.

### 5. Metaphor—Implied or Hidden Comparison

In closing the lesson, broaden the scope of the learners' understanding by using a metaphor or story. This allows the concept to be viewed from a wider perspective such as how it applies to other areas of instruction, to the learner's world at home, or to life in general. These connections can be made through direct metaphors, using similes, analogies, fables, fairy tales, or real-life experiences.

See the Appendices for a planning template to help you incorporate engaging practices into your teaching routines. You may also download a copy from my website, EngagingMinds.Net.

## DEBRIEFING AND PROCESSING

Debriefing and processing activities with your students is an act of drawing out the learning from the experience by asking specific, reflective, and open-ended questions. The goal is to uncover personal insights and awareness from others' interpretations and personal understandings of the experience. There are a couple of foundational models in this chapter to serve as a starting place. You may want to use a variety of reflection options to keep your students from predicting your efforts to help them reflect with presence and eagerness in order to uncover learning. You will be armed with a couple of debriefing models with loads of formats and processing ques-

TOO OFTEN WE GIVE CHILDREN **ANSWERS** TO REMEMBER RATHER THAN PROBLEMS TO **SOLVE.**

tions to help you keep your students' discovery process diverse.

It seems like a huge oversight that only a small percentage of educational programs prioritize developing students' competence as experiential learners.[58]

### Through Effective Debrief Processing you can:

- Add value to what is already happening.
- Increase awareness of other perspectives.
- Develop communication and learning skills.
- Help learners clarify, achieve, and even surpass their objectives.
- Use success or failure as a source of learning and development.
- Make benefits tangible and generate useful data for evaluation.
- Improve prospects for the effective transfer of learning.
- Show that you care about what people experience, value what they have to say, and that you are interested in the progress of each individual's learning and development.
- Provide more ways to communicate, learn, and develop.
- Engage everyone fully by involving all learning style preferences.
- Give better access to intuitive and tacit knowledge.
- Stimulate more powerful learning experiences.
- Generate more effective learning from experience.
- Pay more attention to the experience of learning and allow more realistic testing of future plans.
- Increase the range of strategies for the effective transfer of learning.

## "What", "So What", "Now What" A Debriefing Model

Debriefing is the facilitation of a series of questions from the experiential activity used in class. Essentially, the debrief draws the learning out from the experience. Debriefing can be used to assist learning from almost any experience. Start with a reflection question to get the students to describe "What Happened" in the activity. It is this reflecting process that turns the experience into experiential learning. Next, you move the learners into the generalization or "So What" of the experience. When emotions, thoughts, behaviors, or observations are understood in one situation, this understanding can be generalized and applied in other situations. The next phase of this debrief model is the question "Now What?" This allows the students to reflect and identify their most important take away.

Start simple, then go deep: When processing an activity, it is important to begin your processing and discussion with questions that are easy to answer. Once you have them talking, you can begin to ask more reflective questions that will help students to see how the activity ties to the ideas presented in the lesson.

As learners become more proficient at learning from experience, they do not simply acquire new knowledge. They also practice experimenting, sensing and reflecting, and they may well acquire new skills in each of these areas. Through such practice, students become more talented at every stage of the cycle. They become better at learning from experience.

Consider utilizing *Ground Rules* for the students when using a debrief model. Set up a safe environment for sharing emotions from the experience.

**Sample ground rules:**

1. When possible, use a circle format with the class.
2. Always sit up, keep the energy flowing.
3. This a safe place to explore feelings and learning from the experience.
4. Each person has the freedom to say no or pass. / It's okay to listen and not talk (share).
5. One person talks at a time with no interruptions.
6. No put-downs.
7. Everyone belongs in this group.
8. Speak only for yourself.
9. Both feelings and logical ideas are important.

Asking questions gives you the opportunity to dignify and acknowledge students' efforts regardless whether their answer is correct. Keeping your students engaged and accountable, you can probe for more information simply by saying, "Tell me more about that." The goal is to work with students toward greater understanding of both the concept being studied and their own thinking behind the concept. These questions allow you to get a handle on the distinctions or lack of distinctions a student has at this point in their learning.

## Processing Objectives and Questions

It is important that your students understand the objectives in experiential activities. You help your students understand these objectives with your types of questioning. Here are some questioning tips and guidelines.

1. Provide sufficient "wait time."
2. Utilize appropriate non-verbal communication skills.
   - Eye contact
   - Facial expressions
   - Body posture
3. Observe your students for nonverbal behavior and draw information from it.
4. Ask for feeling about specific happenings during the experience.
5. Be an active listener.
6. Involve reluctant individuals but respect silence.
7. Ask open-ended questions rather than closed.
8. Use directed questioning to highlight issues, roles, and behaviors.
9. Promote self-discovery rather then tell student how they are functioning.
10. Use humor.
11. Vary the length and intensity of debriefing sessions.
12. Use methods such as journals, dyads, drawings, roleplay, solo reflection, whips, and modeling.
13. Closure-type questions include: What did you learn about yourself? What did you learn about other members? What did you do today that you are particularly proud of? How can you use what you learned today in other situations? What obstacle(s) did you need to manage?

## The Four Fs

The *Four Fs* model is a basic questioning system. Always start with easy questions, then dig deeper to discover meaning and gain insight:

**Facts:** *What happened? What specific behaviors or facts can be compiled?* What seemed to work well for you? What didn't work well?

**Feelings:** *What feelings surfaced and how were they expressed?* Was there anything that frustrated you or bothered you? What did you feel good about?

**Findings:** *What can be learned from this experience? How does it relate to what we are learning?* In what ways is this like life?

**Future:** *How might this experience be useful in the future? How can we apply this in our lives?* How does this relate to you? What can you learn from this?

Check out the creative debriefing formats in the Appendix. They will add depth and variety to your debriefing skills. You will appreciate the diversity in your students' responses. They will appreciate the opportunity to discover their best selves.

Consider these final words in your final planning and infusing engaging practices into your teaching philosophy.

## PUTTING IT ALL TOGETHER

Every teacher's experience is unique and every classroom is different. Engaging teachers—no matter where or whom you teach—all have much in common. *Engaging Practices* and its engagement model are based on active learning with the intention to promote skills, strategies, and mindsets that deliver a Bold, Confident, and Prepared class every time.

*Engaging Practices* uses active discovery learning options to expand your learners' knowledge, understanding, familiarity, empathy, and capabilities. By infusing active learning philosophies into everyday content, you'll expand your students' ability to practice or develop a skill set in a safe, neutral learning environment. Students can transfer this learning into their relationship negotiations and content-processing abilities. The engagement model produces more effective learning than passive learning or sit-and-get instruction. Your goal is to intersperse lectures/lessons and reading assignments with active-learning experiences.

Remind yourself that students bring an assortment of rich experiences to class. You design and adapt state changes, engagers, or experiences to ensure easy adjustments that fit different age levels and to incorporate relevant experiences. Effective learning is relevant to your student's life. Your use of simulations and roleplay increases the link between learning and the real world. Keep in mind that many students are driven by egocentric self-needs. Avoid forcing all students to participate in every activity. Offer the choice to opt out. If they take you up on opting out, have a backup responsibility available so the student remains engaged in the activity. Your students' reaction to the class is shaped by expectations related to the content area, class format, fellow students, and you. Establish ground rules that reward risk-taking among students. Promote unconditional positive regard by applauding and acknowledging students for their effort.

We all know different students learn in different ways. These engaging practices accommodate a variety of learning styles and preferences. Make sure your students can respond by writing, speaking, drawing, or acting out a concept. Encourage and permit students to learn individually, in pairs, and in teams or groups. Learn to use a variety of teaching approaches for different types of content and objectives. Learners master skills and knowledge at the level at which they are required to respond during the learning process. If your classroom activity requires students to merely talk about a procedure, help the students apply their experience to their own lives. If you want students to solve problems, the learning activity should require them to solve problems. Avoid trivial, closed questions with rote-memory answers in your engager games. Challenge students with authentic reasoning that requires innovative solutions.

Students learn to repeat behaviors that are rewarded. Make sure that your activities provide several opportunities for gratification and require students to make frequent decisions and responses. During the initial stages of the class, reinforce even partially-correct answers.

Events that are accompanied by intense emotions result in long-lasting learning. Make sure that emotions don't become too intense and interfere with learning. Debrief students after emotional activities to reflect on their feelings and learn from their reactions. Use these engaging characteristics to set this tone:

- **Enthusiastic:** exhibits a zest for life.
- **Commanding:** mobilizes people.
- **Positive:** sees the opportunity in every moment.
- **Personable:** builds rapport easily with a variety of students.
- **Humorous:** appropriately lighthearted about mistakes.
- **Flexible:** finds more than one way to reach outcomes.
- **Accepting:** looks beyond outward actions and appearances to find core values.

- **Articulate:** communicates clearly, succinctly and truthfully.
- **Sincere:** has positive intentions and motives.
- **Spontaneous:** can go with the flow and still maintain outcomes.
- **Interesting and Interested:** connects information to students' life experiences and cares about who the students are.
- **Holds student "able":** believes in and is instrumental in students' success.
- **Sets and maintains high expectations:** establishes guidelines for quality of relationships and quality of work that requires everyone's best effort.

### Action Guide Checklist

A frequent review of the action guide checklist below will assist you in preventing pitfalls. For example, if each set of directions is well-prepared, the class should flow more smoothly. If state changes have been selected and set for certain times during the lesson, you will be less likely to run out of ideas in front of the room. Taking time to review your personal checklist prior to each class may become a useful, even essential, component of your preparation.

- ☐ Has the instruction been structured to work for all learning styles?
- ☐ Is the beginning powerful enough to grab their attention?
- ☐ What engager will be used to start the class/group?
- ☐ What frame positioning statement will be used to create a useful orientation to the class/group?
- ☐ How will the directions be given for each activity?
- ☐ Which state changes will be used during this class/group?
- ☐ How will balance be maintained through "Press & Release?"
- ☐ Where will these state changes be placed in the sequence of

instruction?

- ☐ What role will music play during this topic?
- ☐ Have the social needs of the class/group been appropriately addressed?
- ☐ In what ways will students receive acknowledgment during this class/group?
- ☐ Which labels should be used or avoided in this class?
- ☐ How will resources (if needed) be distributed?
- ☐ What are key linguistic options to be considered?
- ☐ Has sufficient movement been included throughout the day?
- ☐ Is there balance between action, discussion, and reflection?
- ☐ How will positioning statements of open loop be used (curiosity/foreshowing), if at all?
- ☐ Have metaphors and stories been woven throughout the class?
- ☐ How will the key learning points be made memorable?
- ☐ What metaphor, story, or verbal instruction will be used to end the class?
- ☐ Has sufficient time been included for review?
- ☐ Is the ending powerful enough to close the day with a punch?

A simple way to ensure you are including the majority of the key ideas when preparing an engaging class is to review these relevant concepts so that you generate the maximum possible lasting impression for your students.

## Closing Thoughts

Katrina Schwartz[59] says it well: "The scientists can give you certain laws about learning, but they can't put it together into instruction." They understand the neuroscience, not how to translate it into a classroom environment. That's why Schwartz believes the most important thing for good instruction is for the teacher to be an "adaptive expert," someone who is constantly reflecting and learning from what he or she has tried in the past. Adaptive experts have growth mindsets about their teaching, whereas "routine experts" get good at one way and repeat it over and over.

**GOOD TEACHERS ARE ALWAYS LEARNING FROM THEIR STUDENTS.**

I have offered you an engagement model loaded with techniques and how-tos that will fit nicely with your growth mindset and adaptive strengths. Having your instruction misfire feels frustrating to all educators, but it also reaffirms the importance of expertise in the classroom. Consider these engaging practices with your instructional decisions: this model embraces your adaptive expertise!

I concede that being an engaging teacher takes initial planning and prep. I liken it to a space shuttle. When the space shuttle first lifts off the ground, it uses several engine boosts to get out of our atmosphere. Once in space, the shuttle drops a few engines and only uses gentle bursts to move. The same works in your class. Adopt an engaging practices mindset, keep your best, and change the rest!

# A Personal Note to Teachers

Now that you have finished this book, if you have taken a course with me you will know this next comment. Add ONE thing, ONE strategy, ONE method: using positioning statements, incorporating social-emotional learning opportunities, employing engagers as needed, applying a variety of state changes, upgrading your direction giving, or even strategic use of music. I can appreciate you wanting to incorporate all your new learning at one time. Be warned, you are more likely to be successful when you master one engagement practice at a time.

Ask yourself:

- Will what I am about to do or say bring me closer to my students?
- Is what I am doing going to connect to the students' self-interest?
- Would I want to be a learner in my own classroom?
- How am I prepared to teach using active learning strategies?

### Act "As If"

Act as if everything you desire is already here. Whatever your ideal is, picture that image. Then, on a moment-to-moment basis, act "as if" you already are that teacher. Breathe in, breathe out, gain perspective—what does that engaging teacher look like?

Act "as if" you are this teacher, and sooner than you think, you won't be acting anymore. Where the attention goes the energy flows.

"Don't bother just to be better than your contemporaries or predecessors. Try to be better than yourself." - William Faulkner

**Circle of Strength**

Choose to be in close proximity to people who are empowering, who appeal to your sense of connection, and who see the greatness in you. It's amazingly powerful to have the support of a strong, motivated, and inspirational group of peers.

**Be You, Be the Best <u>YOU</u> Imaginable:**

Have a rigorous personal development plan – Invest in yourself
Read the best authors.
Be curious…about everything!
Surround yourself with "Better" people.
Craft your plan to sharpen your own skills.
Take enormous risks!
Brace for obstacles and bounce back.
Take responsibility for your losses.

The universe is waiting for us to show up. Show up and reap the sweet rewards of bringing vitality back to your teaching.

## APPENDIX A

### LET'S TALK MUSIC PLANNING TIPS

Music that truly engages our attention usually features contrasts in volume, inflection and even pacing. Speech that holds the listener's attention is much the same. It rises and falls in volume, it speeds up and slows down, and the best voices resonate.

Additional studies have concluded that music of a certain tempo is best for improving performance and boosting motivation. Not surprisingly, fast-paced music somewhere between 125 and 140 beats per minute (bpm) ("Beat It" by Michael Jackson at 139 bpm is one example) is considered optimal. The effect acts like a stimulant that boosts endurance. Transferring this to the classroom is easily used with an engager (see examples of engagers in the Appendix B) or physical state change.

**RIGHT MUSIC MOTIVATES...**

**WRONG MUSIC AGITATES.**

| Behind The Scenes - Questions & Considerations | |
|---|---|
| **Tone**<br>What is the tone I want to set for this class? | **Thematic Ideas**<br>What messages will the lyrics send to my students? How can I use the songs to build a culture of collaboration? |
| **Genre**<br>What type of music do the students seem to like? | **Beginning of Class**<br>Upbeat – set the tone |
| **Reaction**<br>What is the reaction of the students when they hear music? | **During Movement**<br>Upbeat & Familiar |
| **Volume**<br>What is the reaction of the students to the volume? | **During Discussion or in Background**<br>Music without lyrics<br>60 to 80 Beats Per Minute<br>http://songbpm.com |
| **Personal**<br>What will help energize me as I prepare for the class? | **Exiting of Class, or Unit**<br>Songs about Goodbye, Future, etc., |

Figure 9: Behind The Scenes Music Considerations

### Thematic Options in Music - Making Music Match Content

Choosing songs to match your content or themes in the classroom can be highly rewarding. When auditory-prone students begin to notice that your music is matching the content you are teaching, they usually get excited and will let you know they are noticing what you are playing. I've used the following songs with all age groups.

## Song examples to jumpstart your imagination
### Thematic matching options:

| | |
|---|---|
| First song of the day | Zip-A-Dee-Doo-Dah by Disney |
| Writing/Journaling/Reflection – | **Unwritten** Natasha Bedingfield |
| Math | **ABC** Jackson Five, **1234** Feist, **Rikki Don't Lose That Number** Steely Dan |
| Snack or lunch break | **Yummy, Yummy, Yummy** Ohio Express |
| Use this after lunch or after the holidays | **Welcome Back** by John Sebastian, **What a Difference a Day Makes** Dinah Washington |
| Complimenting others | **'I Like It** Gerry and The Peacemakers |
| Pairing students | **Happy To Be Stuck With You** Huey Lewis and The News |
| Ending the day | **So Long, Farewell** from *Sound Of Music*, **Bye, Bye, Bye** NSYNC, **Hit The Road Jack** Ray Charles, **Who Let The Dogs Out** Baja Men, **Stay** by Maurice Williams |

## Fifteen Faves – A Mix Of Old And New Celebration Songs

1. *Life is a Highway* (Rascal Flats)
2. *Higher* (Taio Curz & Travie McCoy)_
3. *Walking on Sunshine* (Katrina & The Waves)
4. *All Star* (Smash Mouth – Shrek Soundtrack)
5. *I'm A Believer* (Smash Mouth – Shrek Soundtrack)
6. *Do You Believe in Magic* (Aly & AJ)
7. *Good Times* (Chic)
8. *Happy* (Pharrell Williams)
9. *Celebration* (Kool & The Gang)
10. *Life* [Radio Edit] (Haddaway)
11. *Good Feeling* (Flo Rida)
12. *Club Can't Handle Me* (Flo Rida)
13. *Best Day of My Life* (American Authors)
14. *HandClap* (Fitz and The Tantrums)
15. *CAN'T STOP THE FEELING!* (Justin Timberlake Original Song from DreamWorks Animation's "Trolls")

# APPENDIX B

# CHECK OUT THESE ENGAGERS

Some of these engagers will quickly become your classroom favorites and can easily be repeated throughout the year. These can be used with almost all age groups. Feel free to adapt situations or change rules to create more student ingenuity, student participation or interactions.

1. **Alphabet Game** - Everyone stands or sits in a circle. One student starts by throwing an imaginary "A" to another player. That player throws an imaginary "B" as quickly as possible to someone else. And so on. If you have a large class, you can divide them into two circles, call them Team Gold and Team Silver, and time how fast they can get to "Z."
**Variation: Counting Game** - Everyone stands or sits in a circle. One student starts by throwing an imaginary "1" to another player. That player throws a "2" to someone else as fast as possible. And so on.

2. **Add-ons** - This is a fun way to review a topic. One person comes to the front of the room and acts out something they've learned in the class, topic, or course of study. Another one comes up and joins in. Keep adding on until you have five to six people involved, then start a new scene. Could also be done as a living sculpture.

3. **All My Neighbors** - The group forms a circle with chairs. One

person, standing in the middle, does not have a seat. The person in the middle completes the sentence "All my neighbors who..." and anyone who matches the description must find a new seat while the person in the middle finds a seat as well. Later, introduce a variation: "All my neighbors who or have ever..."

**Variation: Get Up and Move** - Make a circle large enough for everyone in the group, except for one person. The person standing says, "Get up and move if..." filling in the blanks with a phrase of his or her choice. For example, "Get up and move if you watch Survivor religiously." After the person makes the statement, everyone it applies to gets up and changes chairs. The one remaining standing makes up a new phrase and the game continues.

4. **Ball Toss Variations** - Five to seven participants stand in a circle about ten feet apart, facing each other. One has a ball or beanbag. She/he tosses the object to a person to start the game. Content could be a Q & A or just to continue a story, give a compliment, word association, math facts, or states and capitals. Keep the game fast and light. Give students control with clear rules.

5. **Back-to-Back Stretches** - Students of about the same size pair up and stand back to back. They hook arms from behind with their backs touching each other. Then on command they are to gently bend forward and stretch each other onto their backs. Caution, safety and gentle back stretching is strongly urged from the beginning. The students exchange back-stretches back

and forth for twenty to thirty seconds.

6. **Camera (Shutter Sound)** - Everyone finds a partner. One person is the "Photographer" and the other is the "Camera." The Camera closes their eyes and the Photographer leads them to a location. When the Camera is in position, their shoulders are squeezed, and they blink their eyes open to take a picture. Repeat with new images. Switch roles.

7. **Circle "Run-Ons"** - All stand in their groups or teams, facing the group leader. The audience is given a topic for review. The group leader starts a sentence but leaves it hanging, such as "Engagers are best for...". The person to his/her left or right, continues the sentence, but again leaves it hanging for the next person. The goal is to keep the sentence running for as long as possible. The one who ends the sentence gets an acknowledgment from the group and begins another "run-on" sentence.

8. **City Night Sounds** - One team at a time picks a group of sounds that might be heard in a big city. On stage, they begin to make their sounds, then add other teams, until you have the sound of a full city. Then initiate a round of applause

for all. Other options include a school, conference, or jungle.

9. **Clapping Rhythms** - As the teacher, start a clapping pattern or rhythm; students or participants repeat it. Once it has traveled around the room, then another student starts a new rhythm. The first person to follow the initial rhythm starts another clapping rhythm and the class follows suit.

**Variation:** Use a pattern, they listen and repeat the pattern. This engager is good for memory, music skills, or for group or teamwork.

10. **Colgate Groupings** - Group forms a mass. Everyone thinks of their brand of toothpaste. On cue, people loudly call out their toothpaste—repeatedly—and gather up in similar groups. Instructor elicits each group's name. Repeat with "Favorite Midnight Munchie," "Dream Car," "Dream Vacation Location," and other age-appropriate ideas.

11. **Count to Ten** - Group forms a circle. Everyone looks at the floor. On the cue "Begin," someone in the group says "One," then someone else says "Two." If two people speak at the same time, the group begins again. The object is to count to ten without overlapping or numbering off sequentially around the circle. Remind them that they do not get to cue each other.

12. **Commercial Breaks** - Each team chooses (or is assigned) a topic related to the material they've been learning. Teams will need some planning time. Throughout the class, different teams offer an impromptu thirty-second TV commercial break. The point of each commercial is to review content and interest the audience in a related service or product. Although this works well with teams, it can, depending on the group, be done with individuals or partners. Encourage students to make their commercials fun and playful.

13. **Creative Handshakes** - The whole class gets to stand up. Then they must introduce themselves to others and find a new way to shake five different people's hands. This builds creativity.

14. **Expert Interviews** - All students stand up. All get new identities: half the participants become an expert in the topic you're teaching and half are famous reporters doing the interviewing.

Take two minutes to get the story, then reverse the roles with another party. Make it dramatic with music. Experts and reporters then debrief the experience with each other.

15. **Finger Joust** - Finger jousting is a sport similar to thumb wars. Two people hold hands like they are arm wrestling and extend their index fingers. The objective of the game is to try and poke the opponent in the shoulder while keeping their hands clasped, not letting it go. Remember to play respectfully.

16. **Frisbee (or Nerf Ball—something soft) Review** - Whoever catches the Frisbee (or object), says one thing that they've learned, or they answer a question given by the teacher related to something the students are learning. Note: after the first time, students learn to avoid the object, so add a point assignment for something special, such as a group popcorn party.

17. **Future Party** - This is a next-step activity, great for setting up presentations. Visualization followed by acting (pretending) a future result. Everyone stands; you lead them through a quick summary of the course learning's. Then take them into the future by one to three months. Ask them to think about presenting their project. In their visualization, it's successful; everyone loves what they presented and how they presented it. Then take them into the future by six months. It's a reunion of everyone currently in the room. They are pleased and surprised to see all these faces. They open their eyes and go around reintroducing themselves and sharing successful stories of what occurred since the end of the presentation. Your music starts out low-key and ends in "Hallelujah chorus."

18. **Hand Hacky** - Create small groups of students. Once in groups, hand out one hacky sack per group. Have students stand with their palms up toward the ceiling. Ask the students to bat the hacky and keep it in the air. Pause the activity to add a step— have the groups clap in celebration when the hacky hits the ground. Pause the activity again to add another step—have the students count how many times they hit the hacky in the air. Pause the group another time to check on how many times they are keeping the object in the air. Then have the groups try for personal bests on the number of times they can keep the hacky sacks airborne.

19. **High Fives** - Instructor models hand gestures including High Fives, Low Fives, High Tens, Low Tens, High Threes, Low Sevens and Behind-The-Back Tens. After students practice with a partner, they have 30 seconds to give a unique kind of High Five to every member of the group. Students create their own high five/fist bump versions.

20. **Instant Replay** - Group forms a circle. One member starts by saying their name and doing a body motion at the same time. The group imitates (like a digital video replay) exactly what each person does, noting vocal tone and body movement. Each person in the circle takes a turn.

21. **Line or Circle Dancing** - Or square dancing with new vocabulary words to learn. Get a dance leader to make it fun…invent your own versions for your content.

22. **Look Up** - Group forms a circle. Everyone looks down at the middle of the floor. When the instructor says, "Look up," everyone looks up directly at one person. If two people are looking at each other, they step out of the circle. Object is to be the last person.

23. **Meet Three People Who** - Teacher completes the sentence "Meet Three People Who . . ." and adds a characteristic, such as "are wearing the color blue," or "have more hair on their head than you do," or "have an 'A' in their name." Repeat with variations.

24. **Mill Mill** - Students form a huddle. Once the students are in the group huddle, teach the students how to mill. In order to mill, instruct the students to drop their heads and cross their arms across their bodies while they are milling among and through the huddle repeating the words "Mill Mill" out loud. After milling is introduced and practiced, the group "mills" among each other until told to pause. After the pause, each student in the group is instructed to  complete a task respectfully on another student near them in the huddle. These are the various commands: With one hand respectfully touch the color blue on somebody else. Staying connected and with the other hand respectfully touch a lighter color on someone else. This can be an uncomfortable engager; don't leave the students touching each other for very long. Say the word 'break' quickly after the last touch directive. Then instruct the group to go back to milling. Perform the milling for 3 rounds. Tell them to pause, and use these other options for the other rounds: "Touch a white shoe," "Touch the cuff of the pants near someone else," "Touch a cool piece of jewelry," "Touch a cool watch or smart watch," "Touch a cool hair doo," Touch elbows with someone else." After the three rounds

are completed have the students give each other high fives and say well done! This engager will need a small debrief due to the physical awkward nature of the physical contact.

25. **Movement of the Masses** - Have students stand up and walk fast or run around the entire ground floor of the building to get their circulation up. As a review, while moving they are to tell ten others some keywords from the last half hour. Set a few rules first about safety, time, courtesy, and noise.

26. **Time Machine** - All students stand up and close their eyes. Turn the clock back twenty, thirty, fifty, or 100 years...how would you talk? Discuss topics you would hold conversations about during that era. What objects would or wouldn't be in the room?

27. **Pair & Share** - Students pick a partner. Share with your partner any of the following (or your own choice): (1) something you are afraid of learning, (2) something you are unsure about, (3) something you found interesting, or (4) the idea just learned.

**Variation Pair & Share - Famous Pairs** - Students pick a partner based on famous pairs. Examples can include: Macaroni & Cheese, Batman & Robin, Laverne & Shirley, Peanut Butter & Jelly, Romeo & Juliet, Bread & Butter, \Cut & Paste, Fish & Chips, Salt & Pepper, Soap & Water, Bow & Arrow, Ying \& Yang, War & Peace, Jack & Jill, Ball & Bat, Green Eggs & Ham, Cookies & Milk, Fork & Spoon, Bagels & Cheese, Ben & Jerry, Apples & Oranges, Hansel & Gretel, Pen & Pencil, Peaches & Cream, Hens & Chicks, Cheese & Crackers, Pizza & Wings, Tom & Jerry, and Lilo & Stitch. You can use

"Famous Pairs"anytime you want students in pair share discussions. The variety of using famous pairs works for getting into pairs or choosing who goes first adds a bit of fun and novelty.

28. **Poster/Flip Chart Art Tour** - Stand up and find a partner. Look around the room and visually pick out two or three posters you like. Take your partner with you and walk over to the posters. Tell your partner why they hit home for you. Why is that one in particular meaningful to you?

29. **Psych Faces** - Students choose between three faces: Rabbit, Walrus, or Moose. Each face has a matching hand gesture. For example, Rabbit has two fingers behind the head, Walrus has tusks using the index finger of each hand in the corners of the mouth, and the Moose has antlers, which are the hands behind the head, fingers spread and thumbs touching. Each person secretly decides which face to be as they are standing back-to-back. On the count of three, students turn to face each other; if the animals faces match, they are considered a psychic. The students do three rounds to make a match.

30. **Room Change** - Ask the group to change the design of the room so that all the furniture is facing a new direction with a new front of the room.

31. **Simon Says** - All students stand and do only what Simon (you) says to do. Give instructions to follow, some of them are prefaced with "Simon Says," and other instructions are given without saying Simon Says. Go at a moderate pace. If they make a mistake, keep the students playing, by continually saying simon says your all back in the game. Always make it a win for all, so no one's never really out of the game. Many variations! You can use it as: (1) A listening game for following instructions; (2) A get-to-know-you game, pointing to, or saying, or facing, a

name you call out; (3) A geography game: "Simon says, point in the direction of California or Florida!" (4) A math game: "Simon says, use your body to give me the answer to five plus six," (5) A language-learning game: "Simon says, point to 'su boca' or 'su mano,'" (6) A science game: "Simon says, point to something in this room made of steel/glass/plastic/over twenty years old/ that would have not existed fifty years ago."

32. **Shoulder Massage** - Have the students stand in a circle all facing one direction so they can put their hands on the shoulders of the students in front of them. On command they respectfully begin to rub the shoulders of the person in front of them and give gentle back rubs. This goes on for about twenty seconds and then they turn around a switch so the students are now giving shoulder rubs to the person now in front of them.

33. **Silent Ball** - Students sit on the tops of their desks and toss a hacky sack, koosh ball, or soft Nerf ball around to each other without talking. If the ball drops or someone speaks, that student sits out by sitting in their desk. Engager is played until only one is left.

34. **Song Re-Write** - Teams or groups vote on their (1) Top learning concept from the course and (2) Their favorite childhood song or catchy tune (such as "Twinkle, Twinkle Little Star," "Row, Row, Row Your Boat," the Oreo cookie or Oscar Meyer songs). Teams or groups write out the lyrics on paper. Then they adapt the song, changing the words to help make a point about what they may have learned. As a team, they present (sing) their adapted song to the whole group.

35. **Stories in a Circle** - Groups form a circle in "storytelling" position—tummies to the floor, if age-appropriate. The title of a story is announced. One person begins by creating the first sen-

tence of the story, with each person in the circle building the story by adding one line. Continue for three to four minutes per story. Repeat with a new title. This can be done standing too.

36. **Stretch & Breathe** - The whole group stands up. The stretching can be a slow movement; it can be done with music; a student can lead the stretching; or it can be done to a theme.

37. **Thumb Wrestling** - Divide the group into pairs. The closer in physical strength people are to each other, the better. Ask each person to face their partner and reach out their right hand. Each person joins his/her partner's hand by making a C shape with his or her fingers then clasp their partner's fingers leaving the thumb out of the grip. The thumbs will be right next to each other. Instruct the students to count to three and alternating the thumbs to opposite sides with the count. At three say, "I declare a thumb war." At this point the students are to try to trap their partner's thumb. Best out of three traps win that round. As time permits add the left hand, so that the students are trying to pin both thumbs at the same time Again, as time permits add the a foot. So in essence they are having a thumb war with both hands and trying to trap a foot all at the same time.

38. **Triangle Tag** - This requires groups of four. Three students form a triangle, holding hands, while the fourth stands outside the group and tries to tag the identified person who is "it." The triangle team keeps spinning to avoid having the "it" person tagged!

39. **Unique Quality / Body Talk** - This engager can be done in teams for fun or individually. Students are given an opportunity to think of a unique (can be physical) quality about them-

selves. Then the students demon-strate their unique quality to others in the group. Examples include but are not limited to having double-jointed extremities, rolling tongue, doing a handspring or dance step, rolling eyes, wiggling ears, one-handed clap, and so on.

40. **Untie the Knot** - Use six to ten people per group. The students form a circle facing toward the center. Everyone reaches into the middle and holds on to someone's hand. Repeat with the other hand, joining with a different person. I usually start with the right hand and then the left hand. Then, staying connected, the group must "Untie the Knot." Instead of hands, try it with five-foot sections of rope or cord per pair of students in the room too. This allows for more room to move and untangle themselves.

41. **Value Line/Take a Stand** - Provide controversial topics related to literature, current events, or historical decisions (such as capital punishment). Create an imaginary line or use tape on the floor to divide one side of the classroom from the other. One side of the line represents the opposite viewpoint of the other side. Students "take a stand" by taking a place on the line that best represents their own informed opinion. Students share their stand/opinion.

42. **Walk Across** - You'll need four to six popular dance songs. Split the group in half and direct them to opposites sides of the room. First, direct one person on each side of the room to walk to the other side as creatively as possible, with each side tak-

ing turns upon instruction. Each person walking across to the other side of the room must walk differently than the student who went before them. Play music loudly as they begin to walk across the room. Once all the individuals finish, invite two at a time to walk across, then three, then four, and so on. You can have as much as five or six as the group go. The idea is to let the momentum of the action and participation, go full out. Note: I usually save this one for the end of a unit, semester, or school year, when students are more unified as a group. It can often turn into a fun celebration.

43. **Word of the Day** - Announce the word early in the class. When you use the word, students all jump up and do three jumping jacks, or touch their toes, or do two burpees, whatever action you can think of will work. Then the students sit right back down while you continue on with your instruction. (How? You decide!). Word of caution: use this one sparingly.

# APPENDIX C

## CLOSING SUMMARY ACTIVITIES

**Alphabet Circle Review** - This is a content review consisting of twenty-six lines of dialogue related to topic learned. The first line starts with a given letter (say R). The next line must start with the following letter (S), and so on, until the whole alphabet has been covered. After Z comes A.

**3-2-1 (3-5 minutes)** - At the end of an explanation or demonstration, pass out index cards and have each person write down three important terms or ideas to remember, two ideas or facts they would like to know more about, and one concept, process, or skill they think they have mastered. This activity can help make a transition to the next task and lets you check in quickly on their progress.

**Note to a Friend (5-10 minutes)** - At the end of an explanation or demonstration, pass out a sheet of paper and ask each student to write a note to a friend explaining the process, rule, or concept they have just learned about.

**Sort the Items (5-10 minutes)** - Ask students/participants to place ideas, concepts, or statements in categories defined by the teacher. For example, the teacher might ask "Which statements were based on fact?" and "Which statements were based on inference?"

**12 Word Summary** - In twelve words or less summarize the most important aspects from today's lesson.

**A - B Partner Teach** - Partner A turn to Partner B. Tell your partner the two most important things you have learned so far about...

**Three Words (Less Is More)** - Choose three separate words (not a phrase) that describes what you experienced during the activity. Allow thirty seconds thinking time, then share in a round. This is usually much quicker than doing sentence completion in rounds. And it often happens to be an example of "less is more"—a lot can be communicated in just three words after a bit of thinking time.

**THERE IS ALWAYS A PIECE OF FORTUNE IN MISFORTUNE.**

OUCH!... I STUBBED MY TOE ON A STUPID HIDDEN ROCK!

**Fortunately, Unfortunately** - This is an adapted truth telling activity to uncover student's perception of a lesson/activity. This is an alternating round in which the group tells the story of the last activity, taking it in turns to say just one sentence beginning with "Fortunately..." or "Unfortunately...." Go around the circle one at a time. Allow passing. Students create a balanced view of what happened. This is especially useful when a group seems over-confident or under-confident.

**Write a 140-Character Tweet** - Record a tweet (twenty words or 140 characters max) ready for sending.

**Use Review Cards** - Make different sets of review cards, each color-coded or clearly marked so that you can readily choose a suitable set of review cards to feed into a reviewing system, whether individually, in pairs, small groups, or the whole group. The cards can have review questions, or half sentences, feedback statements, or review tasks.

**Sentence Starters** - Rounds can be pitched at any level. By trying out different sentence starters, we can find the level at which learners are the most willing and able to take part. Advantages of sentence starters over simple Q&A questions include requiring less thinking (half the answer is supplied), producing clear statements (full sentence answers) and regular repetition to keep answers to the point.

**Sentence Starter Samples:**

The high point for me was when...

The low point for me was when...

The hardest thing for me was...

The easiest thing for me was...

What surprised me was...

Something I knew would happen was...

Nobody listened when...

I'm really pleased that I...

I wish I had...

I felt like going home when...

If I'd had a camera...

If I could do it again I would...

What I found difficult, easy, interesting, satisfying...

I wish I had been asked...

I was annoyed when...

My motivation went down when...

My motivation went up when...

I was helped by...

I helped...

I appreciated...

I was appreciated by...

I'd like to complain to...

I'd like to congratulate...

One last thing I'd like to say is...

What I learned...

What I'm beginning to learn is...

CONVERSATION LEADS TO
COMPREHENSION

# APPENDIX D

## GENERATING SOCIAL-EMOTIONAL OPPORTUNITIES

I have identified the social-emotional skills we are striving to strengthen; now let's talk about some ways we can do this. You can create learning opportunities that promote your students' Psychological Capital. The value of using these activities in supporting social-emotional mindfulness does not just depend on what they experienced during an activity, but on the kinds of connections that are made with other experiences.

These actions show that you care and are interested in your students' personal lives. When you connect with students, they feel recognized and valued. When they feel valued, they trust you. Teaching social-emotional mindfulness requires trust. The more your students feel recognized and valued, the more they grow their efficacy, hope, optimism, and resiliency.

**Using Names** – It turns out that when we use names it helps make each student feel important. It really sends a message that they are important to you and that you care about them.

*Using names explicitly communicates value.*

**Show and tell** – Share personal stories and information about yourself so that students can get to know you and feel that you are approachable.

*When you share information about yourself, you are inviting students into your world. This often makes it easier for them to let you into their world.*

**Token/Reminders** – Give them a personal token or gift. It can be positive quote or object that serves as a reminder of an idea you have been teaching them.

*This is a very simple way to give students a symbolic reminder that you value and care about them. It can also be a wonderful way to reinforce something you have taught them or would like to emphasize.*

**Conspiracies of Kindness** – Perform a random act of service or appreciation for a student with an encouraging note to pay it forward.

*This can be an excellent way to change a student's negative attitude towards the class and can help create a more caring and nurturing environment. One of the greatest ways to increase self-esteem is to serve or express appreciation to another person. This is true whether they are the recipient or the giver of the service.*

**Come Together** – Create a class competition against another class. Instead of competing against each other, this allows the students to work together with a common goal and promotes community. Create a reward for the winning class.

*This can be a great way to get students to work together, support each other, and create class unity. There seems to be more energy and focus when there is a shared purpose among the group of students. Even a very simple reward in this case can serve as a great motivator.*

**Share Your Passion** – Share one of your hobbies, interests, or passions and invite the students to do the same.

*Students become enthusiastic about class when they have the opportunity to share what they love and spend their time doing. It helps them to associate the passion that they feel for those things with the feelings of being in class. It can also be a terrific way for class members and the instructor to get to know one another better. When you know what is really important to a student, you are on your way to establishing a good relationship. Sharing our passions works equally. I had a friend, who was a school counselor. He was also a master pumpkin grower, and would grow pumpkins that were over 300 pounds. He won prizes for his pumpkins. He nurtured them, misted them, played music for the pumpkins, and provided shade when the sun was too hot. Then he would save all the seeds, label them, and give each student a tiny wax paper bag with one seed and the name of the pumpkin that it came from.*

**Post It Note Acknowledgment** – Give a positive personal note at some time during the semester to each student. It could be mailed home or given to them personally.

*This is one of the best ways to send a sincere message outside of class that you care for a student and believe in them. Remember, "a student doesn't really care how much you know until they know how much you care."*

**Personal Interviews** – During the first three to four minutes of class, spotlight a member of the class.

*You may want to have them fill out a questionnaire to gather information. Have a class member read about that individual and then have the class try and guess who it is. This is another great way for students to feel comfortable in the classroom environment and feel like they are a part of the group.*

**Ask Them** – Ask students questions that allow them to express their interests and ideas. Ask them what they like best about school. Ask them about their favorite teachers in the past and why they liked them.

*This gives you an opportunity to see ways that you can improve as their teacher. When people are given the chance to express their opinions it shows that you value their ideas and what they have to say.*

**Skip It, Free Pass, Blues Cards** – Tell the class that you realize that life can be challenging at home, school, or with peers. Because of that, you will give them three (or fewer) blue cards that they can cash in at any time to drop an assignment or a quiz, have extended time on a test or large assignment, or another small "break."

*This is a great way to show that you have empathy for students' challenges. It lets them know that you understand them and care about their personal lives. It allows you to put their interests first.*

**Community Project** – Give something back - Have the class come together for a community project of some kind. The project should be focused on supporting and building-up the community (e.g., gather clothes for the homeless, food drives, blood drives, plant trees, pick-up litter). As the instructor or teacher, take this opportunity to work closely alongside the students.

*When students learn to turn outward in service we often see several positive benefits, including: less depression, and increased gratitude, self-esteem, and motivation. In working with them in a service activity you are in a sense teaching them to do for others without return favor.*

**Two Truths & A Lie** – Share two true stories about yourself and one false one and have the class try and guess which one is false. Allow the class to get to know you a little better.

*This is a very simple way to allow the class to know you, possibly relate to you and makes you approachable. It can be a fun way to make a game of your own story and background.*

**You're the Boss, I Work for You** – Tell the students that this school was built for them. That makes them the boss.

*It's ironic that you are always grading them when they are the real boss here. Give students the criteria for getting an "A" grade in your class. Later ask students to give you the criteria for an "A" grade as their teacher. Ask them to grade your work so far and at different times during the semester.*

**Inspiration Wall** – Set aside a section of a wall or bulletin board, preferably a back wall that isn't used very often, as a personal inspiration wall where each student has something displayed that is personally important.

*Some examples might be a photo with a personal quote, a personal poster. This personal touch builds community and promotes a sense of belonging.*

**Use these Quick Encouraging Statements**

You've discovered the secret

Way to go

I'm proud of you

Fantastic

You're on top of it

Now you've got it

Incredible

You're on your way

Good for you

Remarkable job

Beautiful work

Magnificent

Phenomenal

Creative job

What an imagination

You make me laugh

You brighten my day

You mean the world to me

Awesome

Hurray for you

A high five—a fist pump—a smile

NINE-TENTHS OF EDUCATION IS
# ENCOURAGEMENT

# APPENDIX E

## CREATIVE DEBRIEF OPTIONS

Your students will grow bored with the simple "what," "so what," "now what" debrief format. Mixing up your debrief formats will give you and your students more robust summary disclosures. The personalization will grow with your ability to lead a debrief process differently. Active learning situations with unique yet still insightful debriefs personalize your students' experience.

- *Reflection cards.* Hand out prewritten reflection cards to be used in small groups for a more personal debrief experience.
- *Reflection write.* Use single questions and have the students simply write out their response.
- *Triads with three reflection cards one per person.* Each learner in the triad asks the question to the other two students and so forth with each person in the triad.
- *Small group.* Each small group is given a set of debrief processing questions regarding the experience to lead themselves in a discussion. They answer a set of questions provided to them by you.
- *One-word processing.* This is usually a positive way to have the students summarize their experience into one word, sometimes known as a one-word whip.
- *Wheel within a wheel.* This is the same as inside circle-outside circle. Have the students stand in the outside circle facing inwards. Have another group standing on the inside circle facing outward. Each person will have a partner. One group rotates in one direction while the other group rotates in the other direction. Have a new debriefing/processing question per rotation.

- *Sentence completion.* In addition to the samples in Appendix C, here are a few more.
  - Today I am …
  - A wish of mine is to …
  - My friends are …
  - Something I worry about …
  - Love is …
  - I get upset when …
  - The hardest thing for me to do is …
  - Something I wish people would understand about me is …
  - Other people see me as …
  - I feel important when …
  - What surprised me was …
  - I'm really excited that I …
  - I'd like the group to tell me …
  - One last thing I'd like to say is …
- *Fish bowl.* This is when a smaller group or a pair comes to the front or middle of the room and all the rest of the leaners sit on the outside of the small group to watch and observe from their seats, creating a fishbowl of watching the inside group answer the debriefing/processing questions.
- *Video record and review.* Students video the activity and respond to processing questions regarding what they viewed in the recording.
- *Freezing the moment.* Sometimes you may want to stop or freeze a learning activity when you see individuals or the group at a heightened emotional level. Ask the group for their opinions and observations of that moment. What is happening at this moment? What are your feelings right now, in a word? What are you experiencing right now? What is going on with you right now?

- *Using handicaps.* When your groups work really well together, sometimes adding handicaps (blindfolds, use an arm sling, tie legs together) offers the groups new and unforeseen challenges that up the difficulty of the activity. Note: remind the students to remember the safety rules. This offers new debrief opportunities regarding higher difficulties and how they managed the situations.

  - *Blindfold* – Without vision what was necessary for you to be successful?
  - *Nonverbal* – How did you react to losing a main resource?
  - *Paralyzed* – (Unable to use a limb) What paralyzes you in your class work, friendships?
  - *Siamese* – (Students hooked together) What issues did you have to negotiate to be successful?

- *Metaphor Analogy Challenge.* Metaphors are a mental bridge that links the unknown with the known. Examples include:

  - What are the walls that you face back at home or in other classes and how can you get over them?
  - When in your life do you need to get out of your boat and scout the rapids?

# APPENDIX F

## PLANNING GUIDE

| Course Name | |
|---|---|
| Engager | |
| Frame Positioning Statement (Why) | |
| Activity/Explore/Content | State Changes |
| Debrief / Summary/Closure Activity | |
| Story / Metaphor | |
| | |
| Curiosity-Open Loop Statement setting up anticipation to next session/class | |
| Other Considerations | |

| Time Needed | Props / Materials | Details / Considerations |
|---|---|---|
| | | Music Playlist<br>  Callback song<br>  Content Theme Songs<br>  General Songs<br>  Goodbye Song |
| 1-2 Min | | |
| 30-45 sec / SC | | State Changes<br>  Novelty<br>  Movement<br>  Humor<br>  Resources |
| | | Specific Techniques<br>  Layering<br>  Labels to Avoid<br>  Enrolling Questions<br>  Visual Field |
| | | Room Set up / Climate<br>  Visuals |
| 1-2 Min | |   Inviting Physiology<br>  Signs<br>  Language |

# Endnotes

**Introduction**

1. Adapted from the definition of social-emotional learning skills at www.casel.org.
2. Barbara Fredrickson, *Positivity: Groundbreaking Research Reveals How to Embrace the Hidden Strength of Positive Emotions, Overcome Negativity, and Thrive*, 54-62.

**Chapter 1**

3-4. Diane M. Bunce, et al, "How long can students pay attention in class? A study of student attention decline using clickers," 1442.
5. Rich Allen, *Impact Teaching*, 28.
6. This analogy was updated with 2016 information and taken from Sharon Bowman, *The Ten-Minute Trainer: 150 ways to teach it quick & make it stick!* 1-3.
7. Ibid. 1-3.
8. Flint, "TV networks load up on commercials." http://www.latimes.com/entertainment/envelope/cotown/la-et-ct-nielsen-advertising-study-20140510-story.html Los Angeles Times.
9. Antonio Damasio, *Descartes' Error*, 135-145.
10. Rich Allen, *Impact Teaching*. 33-34.
11. Isen FG.Ashby, "A neuropsychological theory of positive affect and its influence on cognition," 533.
12. Mihaly Csikszentmihalyi, *Finding Flow*, 3-4.
13. Todd Whitaker, *What Great Principals Do Differently*, 27.
14. Howard Gardner, *Multiple intelligences: New Horizons*, 392-393.
15. Benovoy VN.Salimpoor, "Anatomically distinct dopamine release during anticipation and experience of peak emotion to music," 258.
16. Kevin M. Kniffin, "The sound of cooperation: Musical influences on cooperative behavior," 372-390.
17&19. Robert P. Pangrazi, *Dynamic Physical Education For Elementary School Children*, 65 & 91.
18. Rich Allen, *Impact Teaching*. 132.

## Chapter 2

20. Fuhrer A. Marx, "Effects of classroom seating arrangements on children's question asking," 259.

21. Eric Jensen, *Top Tunes for Teaching: 997 Song Titles and Practical Tools for Choosing the Right Music Every Time*, 60.

## Chapter 3

22. Collaborative for Academic, Social, and Emotional Learning. http://www.casel.org/social-and-emotional-learning/.

23. Naomi L Eisenberger, "Does Rejection Hurt? An fMRI Study of Social Exclusion," 292.

24. Jaak Panksepp, "Feeling the Pain of Social Loss," 238.

25. Fred Luthans, *Psychological Capital and Beyond*, 47.

26. Carolyn M. Youssef, "Positive Organizational Behavior in the Workplace: Impact of Hope, Optimism, and Resilience," 792.

27. Michele M. Tugade and Barbara Fredrickson, "Resilient Individuals Use Positive Emotions to Bounce Back From Negative Emotional Experiences," 320.

28. A Rodenberry & K Renk, 2010, 366.

29. Laura Riolli, et al., "Psychological Capital as a Buffer to Student Stress," 1205.

30. Susie CR. Snyder, et al., "Development and Validation of the State Hope Scale," 330.

31. Vicki Zakrzewski, "How to Integrate Social-Emotional Learning into Common Core." https://greatergood.berkeley.edu/article/item/how_to_integrate_social_emotional_learning_into_common_core.

32. Guy Winch, "Why Rejection Hurts So Much – And What To Do About It!" http://ideas.ted.com/why-rejection-hurts-so-much-and-what-to-do-about-it/.

## Chapter 4

33. Venables A. Raine, "Stimulation Seeking and Intelligence: A Prospective Longitudinal Study," 663.

34. Martin EP. Seligman, *Flourish: A Visionary New Understanding of Happiness and Well-being*, 243.

35. Gail T. Fairhurst, "Reframing The Art of Framing: Problems and Prospects for Leadership," 168.

36. Elisabeth Loftus, "Leading questions and eyewitness report," 562.

37. Elisabeth Loftus and JC Palmer, "Reconstruction of automobile destructions: An example of the interaction between language and memory," 587.

38. Gail T. Fairhurst and Sarr. Tversky and Kahneman should be seen as the founders of framing theory, although Fairhurst and Sarr actually coined the term "framing." http://www.valuebasedmanagement.net/methods_tversky_framing.html.

39. Tracey SA, Deetz, et al. *Leading Organizations Through Transition,* 73.

40. Judy Willis, *Research-Based Strategies To Ignite Student Learning,* 40-42.

41. Georgi Lozanov, *Suggestology and Outlines of Suggestopedia,* 61.

42. Alan Nelson, *KidLead: Growing Great Leaders,* 84.

### Chapter 5

43-50. Rich Allen, *Impact Teaching,* 60, 109, 150, 79, 95, 98, 103,176. These pages go into greater detail about the specific techniques that I have used here. I have shared how I use them in my teaching practices.

### Chapter 6

51. George A. Miller, "The magical number seven, plus or minus two: Some limits on our capacity for processing information," 90.

52. Melissa Newberry, et al., *Emotion and School: Understanding How the Hidden Curriculum Influences Relationships, Leadership, Teaching, and Learning,* 25.

53. Manfred Spitzer, Digitale Demenz, http://humanitiesinmedicine.org/manfred-spitzer/ https://www.youtube.com/watch?v=4Ueg55KUQa0.

54. EJ Thomas, "The variation of memory with time for information during a lecture," 61.

55. George A. Miller, "The magical number seven, plus or minus two: Some limits on our capacity for processing information," 90.

56. Laurie S. Glezer, et al., "Adding Words to the Brain's Visual Dictionary: Novel Word Learning Selectively Sharpens Orthographic Representations in the VWFA," 4971.

### Chapter 7

57. Rich Allen, *Impact Teaching,* 188.

58. Peter M. Markulis and Daniel Strang, "A Brief on Debriefing: What it is and what it isn't," 181.

59. Katrina Schwartz, "Why Even Great Teaching Strategies Can Backfire and What To Do About It." https://ww2.kqed.org/mindshift/2017/03/19/why-even-great-teaching-strategies-can-backfire-and-what-to-do-about-it/

# References

Allen, Richard, H. *Impact Teaching*. Needham, MA: Allyn and Bacon, 2002.

Anderson, CA, Carnagey, NL, & Eubanks, J. "Exposure to violent media: The effects of songs with violent lyrics on aggressive thoughts and feeling." *Journal of Personality and Social Psychology*, 84, no. 5 (2003): 960-71.

Andersen, Ole, Marcy Marsh, and Dr. Arthur Harvey. *Learn with the Classics: Using Music to Study Smart at Any Age*. San Francisco, California: LIND Institute, 1999.

Anvari, SH, Trainor, LJ, Woodside, J, and Levy, B.A. "Relations among musical skills, phonological processing, and early reading ability in preschool children." *Journal of Experimental Child Psychology*, 83, no. 2 (2002): 111-30.

Akiyama K and Sutoo D. "Effect of different frequencies of music on blood pressure regulation in spontaneously hypertensive rats." *Neurosci Lett.* 487, no. 1 (2011): 58-60.

Almada, LF, Pereira, A, and Carrara-Augustenborg, C. "What Affective Neuroscience Means for Science Of Consciousness." *Mens Sana Monographs*, 11, no. 1 (2013): 253–273. http://doi.org/10.4103/0973-1229.100409

Ashby, FG, Isen, AM, Turken, AU. "A neuropsychological theory of positive affect and its influence on cognition." *Psychological Review.* 106 (1999): 529-550.

Bamberger, Jeanne. *The Mind Behind the Musical Ear: How Children Develop Musical Intelligence*. Boston, Massachusetts: Harvard University Press, 1991.

Bardo, MT. "Neuropharmacological mechanisms of drug reward: Beyond dopamine in the nucleus accumbens." *Critical Reviews in Neurobiology*, 12 (1998): 37-67.

Berard, Guy, M.D. *Hearing Equals Behavior*. New Canaan, Connecticut: Keats Publishing, 1993.

Bernstein, Douglas A. "Tell and show: The merits of classroom demonstrations." *American Psychology Society Observer*, 24 (1994): 25-37.

Berridge, KC and Robinson, TE. "What is the role of dopamine in reward: Hedonic impact, reward learning, or incentive salience?" *Brain Research*

*Review*, 28, no. 3 (1998): 309-69.

Blood A J and Zatorre, RJ. "Intensely pleasurable responses to music correlate with activity in brain regions implicated in reward and emotion." *Proceeding of the National Academy of Sciences (USA)*, 98, no. 20 (2001): 11818-23.

Bowman, Sharon L. *The Ten-minute Trainer: 150 Ways to Teach it Quick & Make it Stick!* San Francisco, CA: Pfeiffer, 2005.

Bransford, John D., Ann L. Brown, and Rodney R. Cocking, eds. *How People Learn: Brain, Mind, Experience, and School.* Washington, DC: The National Academies Press, 1999.

Brewer, Chris. *Music and Learning: Seven Ways to Use Music in the Classroom.* Tequesta, Florida: LifeSounds, 1995.

Brouchard, R, Dufour, A, and Despres, O. "Effect of musical expertise on visuospatial abilities: Evidence from reaction times and mental imagery." *Brain and Cognition*, 54, no. 2 (2004): 103-9.

Bruer, JT. "Points of View: On the Implications of Neuroscience Research for Science Teaching and Learning: Are There Any?" *CBE Life Sci Educ* 5, no. 2 (2006): 104-110.

Bunce, Diane M., Elizabeth A. Flens, and Kelly Y. Neiles. "How long can students pay attention in class? A study of student attention decline using clickers." *Journal of Chemical Education*, 87 (2010): 1438-43.

Burns, JL, Labbe, E, Arke, B, Capeless, K, Cooksey, B, Steadman, A, and Gonzales, C. "The effects of different types of music on perceived and physiological measures of stress." *Journal of Music Therapy*, 39, no. 2 (2002): 101-6.

Chan, AS, Ho, YC, and Cheung, MC. "Music training improves verbal memory." *Nature*, 396, no. 6707 (1998): 128.

Collaborative for Academic, Social, and Emotional Learning (CASEL). Accessed April 27, 2017. http://www.casel.org/social-and-emotional-learning/.

Csikszentmihalyi, M. *Finding Flow*. New York: First Harper Perennial, 1991.

Damasio, Antonio, interview by Conor Liston, *The Harvard Brain*, 8 Spring (2001).

Damasio, A. *Descartes' Error: Emotion, Reason, and the Human Brain*. New York, NY: Penguin Books, 2005.

Diamond, Marian. *Enriching Heredity: The Impact of the Environment on the Anatomy of the Brain*. New York, NY: Free Press, 1998.

Diamond, Marian, and Janet Hopson. *Magic Trees of the Mind: How to Nurture Your Child's Intelligence, Creativity, and Healthy Emotions from Birth Through Adolescence*. New York, NY: Dutton-Penguin Putnam Inc., 1998.

Deetz, SA, Tracey, SJ, and Simpson, JL. *Leading Organizations Through Transition.* Thousand Oaks, CA: Sage, 2000.

Doyle, Kathryn. (2016) Reuters. Upbeat music may make people more cooperative, Published August 30, 2016. Accessed April 27, 2017. http://www.reuters.com/article/us-health-management-music-behavior-idUSKCN1152GT.

Draganski B, Gaser C, Kempermann G, Kuhn HG, Winkler J, Buchel C, May A. "Temporal and spatial dynamics of brain structure changes during extensive learning." *J Neurosci* 26 (2006):6314–6317.

Dweck, Carol. *Mindset: A New Psychology of Success, How We Can Learn to Fulfill Our Potential.* New York, New York: Ballantine Books, 2006.

Ebbinghaus, Hermann (1885) *Memory: A Contribution to Experimental Psychology.* Translated by Ruger, Henry A, Teachers College, Columbia University, New York City, NY (1913).

Eisenberger, Naomi I, Matthew D Lieberman, and Kipling D Williams. "Does Rejection Hurt? An fMRI Study of Social Exclusion." *Science* 302, no. 5643 (2003): 290-292, doi:10.1126/science.1089134.

Fairhurst, Gail T. "Reframing the Art of Framing: Problems and Prospects for Leadership." *Leadership* 1, no. 2 (2005): 165-85. DOI: 10.1177/1742715005051857.

Fairhurst & Sarr. *The Art of Framing: Managing the Language of Leadership.* San Francisco, CA: Jossey-Bass, 1996.

Ferrucci, Piero. *The Power of Kindness: The Unexpected Benefits of Leading a Compassionate Life.* New York, New York: Teacher Penguin, 2006.

Fiske, Edward, ed. *Champions of Change: The Impact of the Arts of Learning.* Washington, DC: The Arts Education Partnership and the President's Committee on the Arts and Humanities, 1999.

Flint Joe, May 12, 2014, "TV networks load up on commercials," http://www.latimes.com/entertainment/envelope/cotown/la-et-ct-nielsen-advertising-study-20140510-story.html Los Angeles Times.

Fredrickson, Barbara L. *Positivity: Groundbreaking Research Reveals How to Embrace the Hidden Strength of Positive Emotions, Overcome Negativity, and Thrive.* New York: Crown Publishing, Co., 2009.

Furman, A and Strbac, L. "Music is as distracting as noise: The differential distraction of background music and noise on the cognitive test performance of introverts and extroverts." *Ergonomics* 45, no. 3 (2002): 203-7.

Gardner, H. *Multiple Intelligences: New horizons.* New York: Basic Books, 2006.

Gaser, C and Schlaug, G. "Brain structures differ between musicians and nonmusicians." *Journal of Neuroscience* 23, no. 27 (2003): 9240-5.

Glezer, Laurie S, Maximilian Riesenhuber, Judy Kim, Josh Rule, and Xiong Jiang. "Adding Words to the Brain's Visual Dictionary: Novel Word Learning Selectively Sharpens Orthographic Representations in the VWFA." *The Journal of Neuroscience* 35, no. 12 92015): 4965-4972; doi: 10.1523/JNEUROSCI.4031-14.2015.

Goleman, Daniel. *Emotional Intelligence: Why it can Matter More than IQ.* New York, NY: Bantam Books, 1995.

———*Social Intelligence.* New York, New York: Bantam Books, 2006.

Gregory, A, Worrall, L, and Sarge, A. "The developmental of emotional responses to music in young children." *Motivation and Emotion* 20, no. 4 (1996): 341-8.

Gruhn, W, Galley, N, and Kluth, C. "Do mental speed and musical abilities interact?" *Annals of the New York Academy of Sciences* 999 (2003): 485-96.

Hüther, Gerald. *The Compassionate Brain.* Boston, Massachusetts: Trumpeter Books – Shambhala Publications, Inc, 2006.

Jensen, Eric. *Music with the Brain in Mind.* San Diego, California: The Brain Store, Inc, 2000.

———.*Teaching With The Brain in Mind (2nd ed.).*, Alexandria, VA: Association for Supervision and Curriculum Development 2005.

———.*Top Tunes for Teaching: 997 Song Titles and Practical Tools for Choosing the Right Music Every Time.* San Diego, California: The Brain Store, Inc, 2005.

Katz, Mark. *On Playing a Poor Hand Well.* New York: Norton & Company, Inc., 1997.

Kniffin, Kevin M, Jubo Yan, Brian Wansink, and William D Schultze. "The sound of cooperation: Musical influences on cooperative behavior." *Journal of Organization Behavior* (2016): 1099-1379. http://dx.doi.org/10.1002/job.2128.

Loftus, EF. "Leading questions and eyewitness report." *Cognitive Psychology* 7 (1975): 560-572.

Loftus EF, Palmer, JC. "Reconstruction of automobile destructions: An example of the interaction between language and memory." *Journal of Verbal Learning and Verbal Behavior* 12 (1974): 585-589.

Lozanov, Georgi. *Suggestology and Outlines of Suggestopedia.* New York: Gordon and Breach, 1978.

Luthans Fred, Carolyn M Youssef-Morgan, and Bruce J Avolio. *Psychological Capital and Beyond.* New York: Oxford University Press, 2007.

Luthans Fred and Carolyn Youssef-Morgan. "Emerging Positive Organizational

Behavior." *Journal of Management* 33 (2007): 321–349.

Markulis, Peter M and Daniel Strang. "A Brief on Debriefing: What It Is and What It Isn't." *Developments in Business Simulation and Experiential Learning* 30 (2003): 177-184.

Marx, A, Fuhrer, U, and Hartig, T. "Effects of classroom seating arrangements on children's question asking." *Learning Environments Research* 2, no. 3 (1999): 249-263.

Mendes, Ernie. *Empty the Cup...Before You Fill It Up.* Carlsbad, CA: Mendes Training & Consulting, Inc., 2003.

Merritt, Stephanie. *Mind, Music and Imagery: Unlocking the Treasures of Your Mind.* Santa Rosa, California: Aslan Publishers, 1996.

Miles, Elizabeth. *Tune Your Brain: Using Music to Manage Your Mind, Body, and Mood.* NY, New York: Berkley Publishing Group, 1997.

Miller, George A. "The magical number seven, plus or minus two: Some limits on our capacity for processing information." Psychological Review 63 (1956): 81-97.

Nelson, Alan. *KidLead: Growing Great Leaders.* BookSurge Publishing, 2009.

Newberry, Melissa, Andrewa Gallant, and Philip Riley. *Emotion and School: Understanding How the Hidden Curriculum Influences Relationships, Leadership, Teaching, and Learning.* Bingley, UK: Emerald Group Publishing Ltd., 2013.

Olsen, K. *Science Continuum of Concepts for Grades K-6.* Kent, WA: Center for the Future of Public of Education, 1995.

Ortiz, John M. *The Tao of Music: Sound Psychology.* York Beach, Maine: Samuel Wiser, Inc., 1997.

———. *Nurturing Your child with Music: How Sound Awareness Creates Happy, Smart and Confident Children.* Hillsboro, Oregon: Beyond Words Publishing, 1999.

Pangrazi, Robert P and Aaron Beighle. *Dynamic Physical Education for Elementary School Children (17th ed).,* San Francisco, CA: Pearson, 2012.

Panksepp, Jaak. "Feeling the Pain of Social Loss." *Science* 302, no. 5643 (2003): 237-239, doi: 10.1126/science.1091062.

Peters, Stephen. *Do you know enough about me to teach me?* Orangeburg, SC: Cecil Williams, 2004.

Purkey, William Watson and John M Novak. *Inviting School Success: A Self-Concept Approach to Teaching.* Belmont, CA: Wadworth Publishing Co, 1996.

Raine, A, Venables, PH, Reynolds, C, and Mednick, SA. "Stimulation Seeking and Intelligence: A Prospective Longitudinal Study." *Journal of Personality and Social Psychology* 82, no. 4 (2002), 663-674.

Rhodes RE. "The built-in environment: the role of personality and physical activity." *Exerc Sport Sci Rev* 34, no. 2 (2006):83-8.

Riolli, Laura, Victor Saviki, and Joseph Richards. "Psychological Capital as a Buffer to Student Stress." *Psychology* 3, no. 12A (2012): 1202-07, doi: 10.4236/psych.2012.312A178.

Roddenberry A, and K Renk. "Locus of control and self-efficacy: potential mediators of stress, illness, and utilization of health services in college students." *Child Psychiatry Human Development* 41, no. 4(2010):353-70.

Sabbeth, Alex. *Rubber-Band Banjos and a Hava Jive Bass: Projects and Activities on the Science of Music and Sound.* New York: John Wiley & Sons, 1997.

Salimpoor VN, Benovoy M, Larcher K, Dagher A, Zatorre RJ. "Anatomically distinct dopamine release during anticipation and experience of peak emotion to music." *Nat Neurosci* 14, no. 2 (2011):257-60.

Sapolsky, Robert. *Why Zebras Don't Get Ulcers.* New York: W.H. Freeman and Company, 1994.

Schwartz, Katrina. "Why Even Great Teaching Strategies Can Backfire and What to Do About It." *KQED News.* Published March 19, 2017. Accessed April 27, 2017. https://ww2.kqed.org/mindshift/2017/03/19/why-even-great-teaching-strategies-can-backfire-and-what-to-do-about-it/

Seligman, Martin EP. "Building human strength: Psychology's forgotten mission." *APA Monitor*, 29, no. 1(1998).

Seligman, *Flourish: A Visionary New Understanding of Happiness and Well-being* New York, NY: Free Press, 2011.

Siegel, Daniel J. *The Mindful Brain: Reflection and Attunement in the Cultivation of Well-Being.* New York: Norton, 2007.

Snyder, CR, Susie C Sympson, Florence C Ybasco, Tyrone F Borders, Michael A Babyak, and Raymond L Higgins. "Development and Validations of the State Hope Scale. *Journal of Personality and Social Psychology* 70, no. 2 (1996): 321-335, doi: http://dx.doi.org/10.1037/0022-3514.70.2.321.

Spitzer, Manfred. *Digitale Demenz: Wie wir uns und unsere Kinder um den Verstand bringen.* München: Droemer Verlag, 2012.

Storr, Anthony. *Music and Mind.* New York: Free Press, 1992.

Sylwester, Robert. *How to Explain a Brain: An educator's handbook of brain terms and cognitive processes.* Thousand Oaks, CA: Corwin Press, 2005.

Thomas EJ. "The variation of memory with time for information during a lecture." *Stud. Adult Educ* 4 (1972): 57–62.

Tugade, Michele M and Barbara L Fredrickson. "Resilient Individuals Use Positive

Emotions to Bounce Back from Negative Emotional Experiences." *Journal of Personality and Social Psychology* 86, no. 2 (2004): 320–333.

Tversky, Amos and Daniel Kahneman. "Prospect Theory: An Analysis of Decision under Risk." *Econometrica* 47, no. 2 (1979): 263-291.

Vaynman, S and F Gomez-Pinilla. "Revenge of the 'sit': how lifestyle impacts neuronal and cognitive health through molecular systems that interface energy metabolism with neuronal plasticity." *J Neurosci Res* 84, no. 4 (2006):699-715.

Whitaker, Todd. *What Great Principals Do Differently (2nd ed)*. New York: Routledge, 2012.

Willis, Judy, M.D. *Research-Based Strategies to Ignite Student Learning*. Alexandria, VA: ASCD, 2006.

Wilson, Larry and Hersch Wilson. *Play to Win: Choosing Growth Over Fear in Work and Life*. Marietta, GA: Bard Press, 1998.

Winch, Guy. "Why Rejection Hurts So Much – And What To Do About It!" Ideas. TED.com. Published December 8, 2015. Accessed April 27, 2017, http://ideas.ted.com/why-rejection-hurts-so-much-and-what-to-do-about-it/.

Youssef, Carolyn M and Fred Luthans, Fred. "Positive Organizational Behavior in the Workplace: Impact of Hope, Optimism, and Resilience." Lincoln, Nebraska: Management Department Faculty Publications, 2007. Accessed April 27, 2017, http://digitalcommons.unl.edu/cgi/viewcontent.cgi?article=1035&context=managementfacpub.

Zakrzewski, Vicki. "How to Integrate Social-Emotional Learning into Common Core." *Greater Good*. Published January 22, 2014. Accessed April 27, 2017. http://greatergood.berkeley.edu.

Zatorre, RJ. "Music and the Brain." *Annals of the New York Academy of Sciences* 999 (2003): 4-14.

# Acknowledgments

During my graduate work at Arizona State University, I became fast friends with Rich Allen. The first time I observed him teaching a class, I knew that was the way I wanted to teach. Thank you, Rich Allen, for mentoring me and catapulting my career. I get to live a life that I've designed because I believed you!

Orvel Ray Wilson, CSF, CSP–Your support to start this book helped me get past my fears and realize that writing this book was important. Thank you!

Thank you to Julie Berlin and Jami D. Rodgers for serving as my content editors. Julie Berlin, your feedback and input regarding the Engagement Model was most appreciated. Jamie, your input about adding examples heightened the relevancy of this book.

Thank you to Alexandra O'Connell, my gifted editor, for your expertise and wisdom with the written word. Your help in sculpting my first book is more appreciated than I can express.

To my designer, Andrea Costantine, huge creative thanks! Your expertise has proven invaluable.

And finally, thank you Susie Schaefer, my publish¬ing consultant. Susie, your encouragement and guidance have made this writing process exciting and trouble-free.

# About the Author

## INSPIRING BETTER ENGAGEMENT!

Cristal McGill received her PhD in Educational Psychology from Arizona State University. People who have taken her workshops and classes praise her creative style, innovation, and passion for teaching. She has a reputation for facilitating upbeat, interactive, meaningful sessions marked by engaging instructional practices.

Cristal also facilitates dynamic "train the teachers to be trainers" seminars, allowing her to model and coach engaging practices with school districts that require teachers to provide professional development for their peers.

As a leader in the field of engagement, her workshops are loaded with practical, easy-to-use tips and tricks, a game-changer in professional development experiences. Workshops with Cristal have a consistent record of increasing attendance, cooperation, and participation due to her facilitation of active learning strategies. Cristal offers one-to four-day programs customized to your specific needs. Participants walk away with an "explosion" of ideas guaranteed to lift any classroom to an entirely new level.

If you ask Cristal how she stays resilient, she will give you many reasons, but the one she favors most is her experience as a whitewater river guide. *Engaging Practices* is her first book. Find her at www.EngagingMinds.Net.

66996079R00117

Made in the USA
Middletown, DE
16 March 2018